MW00592971

The Therapy Triangle

Empowering you with the knowledge to heal™

by
Robert Burkham, Ph.D.
Clinical Psychologist

Book & Book Cover Design, Brand Identity Design & Development
Prime Design, Appleton WI

Randall –
It was so good
to meet you and
your family at
your family Happy
graduation.
reaching – if you
have any feedback
my email is
robburkham @gmail.co

Copyrighted Material. All rights reserved.Copyright © 2005 by Robert Burkham, Ph.D.

PREFACE AND DEDICATION

I first sat down to write this book in January of 1994 because there were no books which I could recommend to my clients to guide them through the challenging process of change which is psychotherapy. I wanted to point my clients to a book which would focus on the process of therapy, not just the facts. I wanted a book that would inspire clients to work on what they can change (themselves) and accept what they cannot change(others).

Looking at therapy as an emotional triangle seemed to provide a way to understand and pull together the many aspects of therapy in a way which would be relatively simple, informative, and realistically hopeful. My aim is to inspire you to use psychotherapy well to make the best life that you can for yourself, those close to you, and for the world around you.

This book is dedicated to the thousands of clients I have been privileged to work with since I conducted my first therapy session as a graduate student in the fall of 1976. These brave and often frightened people have taught me more than I could have imagined when I sat down with my first client so many years ago.

This book is also dedicated to my family. My late father, Robert Burkham, and my late mother, Sally Robyn, both passed on to me a love of learning and a tendency to doubt the status quo. My loving and beautiful wife, Terri, strengthens me every day to love life and to live it fully. My four natural and two step-children, Ana, Jon, Deanna, Jen, Jeremy, and Erica, have helped me to grow up even as I have helped them.

The Therapy Triangle

Published by
Right Mind Publishing,
a division of Robert Burkham, Ph.D., S.C.

Copyright © 2005 by Robert Burkham, Ph.D., S.C.
All Rights Reserved

Right Mind Publishing
Appleton, Wisconsin

Library of Congress has established
a cataloging record for this title

Library of Congress Catalog Number 2004094050

ISBN 978-0-9741838-1-7

Printed in the United States of America
First Edition: March 2005

Table of Contents

Chapter 1: **Therapy is Not Surgery**
Page 9

Chapter 2: **What Drives Us to Therapy? Pain, Responsibility, Opportunity and Hope**
Page 23

Chapter 3: **Hoping That Others Will Change and the Birth of the Therapy Triangle**
Page 39

Chapter 4: **Therapists: The Good, the Bad, and the Overly Helpful**
Page 57

Chapter 5: **Differentiation (Part I): Becoming Yourself While Being With Others**
Page 91

Chapter 6: **Differentiation (Part II): How to Maintain the Changes You've Made**
Page 123

Chapter 7: **Potential Aides to Lasting Change: Techniques and Medication**
Page 133

Chapter 8: **Some Questions of Logistics**
Page 163

Chapter 9: **A String of Pearls and a Farewell**
Page 185

Chapter 1

Therapy is Not Surgery

Nora had been thinking about getting help for years but just recently she had begun to feel desperate enough to do it. In the past few weeks, she had experienced terrible fear and hopelessness which would crescendo every few days into full-blown anxiety attacks: she would become short of breath and light-headed, her heart would pound, and her thoughts would race towards seeing herself dying of a heart attack. She began to dread going out in public, fearing that she would have one of these attacks when no one would be there to help. She was 53 now and had experienced a few of these attacks when she was in her early twenties but they had never been so strong.

Nora had recently become extremely frustrated with her husband, Charlie, because he would not talk to her about anything significant or personal. She knew that their marriage had been dying a slow death for many years and she was frightened about their future together. She was also frustrated with Charlie because he was so critical and angry towards their only child, Quinn, who was now 18. Quinn had just recently gone off to college and Nora was worrying about him every day. She told herself over and over that he would not take the medication for his asthma, that he would not get enough sleep, that he would drink too much, and that he would flunk out. Every day Nora woke up to the sound of her own distressing thoughts: she found herself dwelling on how afraid she was for Quinn and how angry she was towards Charlie. She had woken up this way every day for weeks. She would continue to think this way throughout each day except when she was preoccupied by her duties at work

She realized that she needed professional help but she was afraid to seek it out. She had always been able to handle her problems herself and had never wanted to see a "shrink". A few weeks after Quinn left for college, he had a severe asthma attack and ended up in the hospital. Nora became totally obsessed with her worries about Quinn. She felt that there was no way out of her daily agony of anger and fear. She called her best friend Gloria who had needed professional help when she had gone through a very painful divorce. Gloria told Nora that she had seen Dr. Susan Kleinfelter during this difficult time and that Dr. K had been very helpful to her. Gloria gave Nora Dr. K's phone number and, after Nora argued with herself for another week, she called and set up an appointment. She felt ashamed that she couldn't get herself out of her current difficulties by her-self. She felt afraid of what she might find out about herself and her marriage from the doctor. As the appointment approached, she had strong urges to cancel it but she went anyway.

At the appointed hour, she found herself in a small but tastefully decorated waiting room nervously shifting in her seat while pretending to read a magazine. After about ten minutes, a rather petite, professionally dressed, and enthusiastic woman of forty came into the room, smiled at her warmly, shook her hand and said, "Hi, you must be Nora. Welcome. I'm Dr. Kleinfelter. Why don't you come back this way to my office so that we can get started."?

Within the first few minutes of their session, Nora began to pour out her anger towards her husband and her worry about her son. She felt uneasy talking so critically about them to Dr. K, as if she were betraying them to a stranger. At the same time, she hoped that Dr. K would take her side against them and get them, somehow, to make the

changes she knew they needed to make. Even in these first
few minutes, a therapy triangle was beginning to form.

Sigmund Freud began the modern practice of psychotherapy a little over one hundred years ago. Although therapy has changed greatly since the 1890's, every relationship between therapist and client throughout the history of psychotherapy has been part of a triangle of relationships. Because every client is part of a multi-generational stream of humanity called a family, every therapy affects and is affected by the client's family. This is true whether the therapist meets the client's family (as in family or couple therapy) or the therapist never meets any of them (as in individual therapy). Often this triangle goes unrecognized by the patient, the therapist, or both but it still exerts a powerful effect on the success or failure of therapy. In the pages of this book, I will explain how the therapy triangle works so that you can get a clear picture of how treatment can work for you.

Every year more than ten million Americans do what Nora did: begin a relationship with a therapist. Nora came to Dr. Kleinfelter because of anxiety symptoms and family problems but people come to treatment for many other reasons: depression, grief, behavior problems in their children, alcohol and drug problems, anger, marriage problems, divorce, the struggles of caring for aging parents, sexual problems, and stress-related headaches, to name only a few.

As we just saw, Nora was beginning to form a therapy triangle. She was angry and frustrated with her husband and her son but could not successfully deal with her problems with them without outside help. She came to a helping professional because of her anxiety but also because she wanted Charlie and Quinn "fixed" so she wouldn't have such distress. Dr. K felt pressure even early in the first session to take Nora's side against her insensitive husband and her irresponsible son. This web of relationships between the client, the therapist and the client's important family members is the "therapy triangle".

It is always present in therapy; how the members of that triangle handle themselves has a great impact on whether therapy is successful in bringing about lasting changes. Understanding how the therapy triangle forms, how it can prevent lasting change from taking place, and how it can promote lasting change is the subject of this book.

Studies of therapy indicate that of the millions of people who seek out professional help and stick with it for a significant number of sessions, about one-third will be significantly better by the time treatment ends and another one-third will be much better. Thus two-thirds of all therapy clients who stay in therapy will find their symptoms and problems significantly improved. Many of these successful therapy clients will make lasting changes which will improve the quality of their lives for many years to come. However, a substantial number of apparently successful clients will make only temporary changes. Within a year or two of terminating therapy, they will return to the same or similar problems for which they originally sought help. Still other clients will not improve at all with therapy and a very small but significant group (about 5% of the total) will actually get worse.

Research clearly indicates that successful therapy is not cheap or miraculously quick. In recent decades, therapists have made therapy briefer and more effective, but it still takes time. Therapy which lasts from six months to several years and consists of 10 to 50 sessions is not at all unusual. In one recent study which summarized research done on thousands of clients, fully 75% of clients improved if they had six months of once-a-week sessions, 26 sessions in all. While successful therapy takes time, our health care system is currently putting powerful financial pressure on therapists and clients to make therapy as brief as possible. More and more of us have our therapy paid for by health insurance companies which themselves are under increasing pressure to reduce costs. This often means that clients and therapists have fewer sessions available to do the difficult work of helping the client make lasting changes.

THE PURPOSE OF THIS BOOK

This book is designed to help you understand the basic principles and processes of therapy so that you can use treatment as efficiently as possible to make satisfying and lasting life changes. I am presenting the ideas in this book to you, therapy clients and potential clients, who are not trained therapists because I am convinced that therapy is not mysterious; the basic principles that determine whether therapy will be successful or not can be understood by anyone who seeks help. In these pages, I will strive to explain how and why therapy works by examining the three human facets of treatment, which are crucial in determining its success or failure: you, your therapist, and your family. (When I use the term "family" in this book, I refer not only to people who are related to you biologically, by marriage, or by adoption, but also to other people who are very close to you such as live-in partners and foster children).

I will illustrate the ideas presented in these pages with numerous case examples and, throughout the entire book, I will present the story of Nora, Dr. Kleinfelter, and

Nora's family so that the reader can get a detailed picture of how one client, her family, and her therapist struggled to make significant and lasting changes.

THE DEFINITION OF THERAPY

Before we begin discussing the basic principles of psychotherapy, we need a working definition. Most simply, therapy is a relationship between a professional with formal training in helping people overcome problems in thinking, feeling, behavior, and relationships and a person or persons seeking such help. It is often a relationship between one client and a therapist (individual therapy) but is also frequently conducted with a couple (couple therapy), a group of family members (family therapy), or a group of unrelated individuals (group therapy). This book will focus on individual, couple, and family therapy rather than group therapy although many of its principles apply to group therapy as well.

Therapy is a lop-sided relationship because, although you reveal much about your life, the professional reveals little about her or his life. You may present your problems, emotions, struggles, and successes from your personal life; your therapist will give insight, advice, support and challenge. Your therapist earns money doing therapy; you (or your health insurance) usually pay for the therapist's services. The relationship is to be conducted within the bounds of the ethical code of the therapist and is not to be a sexual relationship, a friendship, and it is not to be contaminated by any other business or personal relationship between therapist and client. Professionals are ethically bound not to be therapists to family members, close friends, employees, or business associates.

Most importantly for the purposes of this book,

therapy is a collaborative relationship between you and your therapist. It is a relationship in which the two sides need to work closely with each other to achieve the goal of resolving or at least ameliorating your problems. Therapy is not surgery; it cannot be done to you. You must take an active role in the relationship if you are going to make the changes you want to make.

THERAPY IN HOLLYWOOD AND REAL LIFE

It has been my experience that many clients who are new to therapy get their ideas and images about what actually goes on in treatment not from therapists but from popular culture, most importantly television and the movies.

Hollywood has traditionally presented therapy in either of two ways: it is either magically successful or an absurd waste of time and money.

In the first, the professional wisely guides the client to face a single traumatic event in the past. The client faces the traumatic event with a great outpouring of painful emotion and the result is the rapid and complete elimination of all the client's difficulties. This portrayal reflects a common belief about therapy: all the client needs to do is express or "ventilate" their innermost feelings and their troubles will quickly vanish. This myth about therapy fits well into movies with happy endings but treatment rarely, if ever, follows this pattern. Real therapy is more difficult, involves much more work on the client's part, and progress is much more gradual. Clients' problems rarely stem from one traumatic incident but from pervasive patterns of thoughts, feelings, and behaviors in the client's life which are dealt with a little at a time. Progress is more often than not of the "two steps forward and one step back" variety rather than the dramatic, rapid recovery without setbacks seen in these movies. In real life, the outcome of therapy is usually not as clear as in the happy ending in the movies; the client does not live happily ever after. If treatment is successful, the client goes on to live a more fulfilling life even though he or she continues to struggle with life, as do we all.

If therapy is not being portrayed as magically successful by Hollywood, it is often presented as absurd and unhelpful. The client talks endlessly about their problems with little or no input from the therapist. Occasionally the professional will say "uh-huh" or "I see". When asked a direct question by the client, the therapist turns the tables and says "what do you think?" and the client remains as puzzled as ever about what to do to get better. At the end of the 50-minute hour, the therapist abruptly says "we have to stop for today" or "we'll pick this up next time" and the client leaves the office even more baffled than they were when they entered. In this scenario, treatment goes on forever with the professional getting wealthier and the client getting no help whatsoever. Therapy is a racket and the client is a sucker. In real life, unfortunately, some professionals conduct treatment this way and it is a racket. However, in real life, therapists are usually more helpful and treatment is much more focused. Therapist are actively involved in helping the client understand their thoughts, feelings, behaviors, and relationships and guiding the client towards changes that he or she wants to make.

Recently, Hollywood has begun producing movies in which the therapist has a sexual relationship with the client. These relationships are often portrayed as helpful to the client because they provide them with new insights and hope. In real life, when treatment involves a sexual relationship between therapist and client, the professional is exploiting the client's vulnerability to satisfy their own power needs. Treatment often becomes a repetition of past abuse suffered by the client and as such it is highly destructive. It is unethical and in many states a crime on the part of the therapist.

In all three of these scenarios from Hollywood, the client is essentially passive. In the scenario in which therapy is magically successful, the client simply receives the insight from the therapist and doesn't need to work on their problems. The client's problems evaporate without a struggle. In the scenario in which therapy is absurdly unhelpful, the client endlessly recounts their thoughts, their feelings, and often their dreams but does not take an active role in figuring out their problems or making any changes. The therapist and the client seem to be waiting for the blinding flash of insight but it never comes. In the scenario in which treatment involves a sexual relationship, the client loses sight of her or his problems and focuses on the magically helpful relationship with the therapist. It is magical because it involves no work on the part of the client.

If the client only needed to receive treatment from the therapist, there would be no need for this book. However, in the real world, successful therapy requires the client to have the good judgment to find a competent therapist, the persistence to stay with therapy even when it is difficult, the courage to face painful parts of him- or herself, and the daring to try out new and often feared patterns of thinking and relating to others.

TWO BASIC IDEAS:
THE THERAPY TRIANGLE
AND THE DIFFERENTIATION OF THE SELF

In order for this book to be both succinct and helpful, I have avoided using the jargon for which therapists are so famous. However, there are two concepts, which I will be using throughout the book, which need to be carefully defined so that the ideas presented here will make sense:

1. **The therapy triangle** is the web of relationships between your therapist, yourself, and your family.
2. **Differentiation of self** is the process by which people mature and grow.

The therapy triangle is an example of an "emotional triangle", a set of relationships in which two people cannot resolve a conflict and one of them seeks out the support of a third party. Depending on how maturely the three parties handle themselves, an emotional triangle can become stuck and prevent any resolution of the original conflict or it can help resolve the original conflict. The triangle involving your therapist, yourself, and your family is just such a triangle. It forms naturally and can become stuck, making it impossible for you to make any lasting changes in your life.

On the other hand, skillful work by you and your therapist can get the triangle unstuck and make lasting change possible for you. Knowing how this triangle works can guide you in your choice of a truly helpful therapist and clarify what you need to work on in therapy. Understanding the triangle can also help you grow by learning to relate to your family members in a healthier way. The therapy triangle will be explored fully in Chapter 3.

Differentiation of the self is the process of the growth of a person toward maturity. Becoming more mature does not mean becoming grimmer and less playful about life. It means being more at peace with yourself and more able to relate to others without fear. The more differentiated we are, the more maturely we handle others and ourselves.

There are two types of forces which pull and push on all of us throughout our lives: there are forces which push us away from others and towards becoming separate, independent, and emotionally distinct individuals who can think, feel, and act for ourselves. There are also forces that pull us towards others, propelling us to lose our individual identity in a human group or family and to think, feel, and act as one. The differentiation of the self is a life-long, never-completed balancing of these two forces. Differentiation is the process which, if carried far enough, leads a person to be completely one's own person and yet be able to connect closely with others. No one ever becomes perfectly differentiated so no one is able to be completely him- or herself and yet connect closely with others. There are a few highly differentiated people among us and they are very clear about their purpose and values without trying to force others to adopt those same values. They thoughtfully shape their lives according to their purpose and values and can maintain close and peaceful relationships with the people who are important to them. The highly differentiated person can listen thoughtfully to individuals who are highly critical of them without losing their focus and without trying to force those other people to have the same values and purpose as themselves.

I will be returning often to this idea of differentiation to help you understand yourself and your family, your therapist (Chapter 4), and the process of making lasting changes (Chapters 5 and 6).

WHY SHOULD YOU TRUST THIS BOOK?

One very important question, which I need to address before we move on, is this: how much faith should you put in this book? There are thousands of books about human behavior written by licensed experts such as myself; from my point of view they range from being very credible and helpful to being very misleading and destructive. My ideas are based on four sources:

1. The theoretical writings of most of the major schools of therapy have provided much important information.

2. Modern psychotherapy is just over 100 years old so there is a century of writings by therapists struggling to explain how it works.

3. I have learned from the scientific research about psychotherapy. Researchers point out that psychotherapy is one of the most thoroughly researched professional activities in the world. I have tried to make what I have written here consistent with that research although what I say here goes beyond what research can definitely say to be true.

4. I have been profoundly influenced by the Natural Systems Theory developed by Murray Bowen, M.D. (1915-1990). I have found Dr. Bowen's theory to be

the most comprehensive and powerful theory of human behavior currently available. Dr. Bowen's theory has not only helped guide me as a therapist and as a person but its concepts have been very valuable to the people who have sought my help.

5. I have benefited greatly from my own decades of experience as a therapist. I have learned many challenging and at times surprising lessons from my clients about what is helpful and what is unhelpful in treatment.

From these four sources I have put together the thoughts set forth in these pages. Many therapists will disagree with at least some of what I have to say; fortunately the therapy field is young enough and dynamic enough (even after 100 years!) that there is no accepted doctrine or "party line" to which all therapists adhere. These thoughts are my opinions and so I would advise the reader to consider the ideas set forth here thoughtfully and with a healthy dose of skepticism. Only you can finally evaluate the helpfulness of what is written in these pages.

Pearl of Wisdom: Remember that therapy is a joint venture between you and your therapist; therapy cannot be done to you. Also remember that the connection between you and your therapist does not exist in a vacuum because you are part of a family. How you, your therapist, and your family handle the emotional triangle which forms so naturally will greatly impact how lastingly helpful your therapy will be.

Chapter 2

What Drives Us to Therapy?
Pain, Responsibility, Opportunity and Hope

A colleague of mine once conducted an initial interview with a woman of about 35 who was very unclear about her reasons for seeking help. She vaguely stated that she was unhappy with her weight (although she was not particularly overweight) and equally vaguely stated that she was dissatisfied with her marriage. In her second session, she continued to complain but could not say why she was coming to therapy and what she really wanted. She did not show up for her third session and my colleague called her to remind her of her appointment and to ask why she had not shown up. She stated matter-of-factly that she could not come to therapy any more. When my colleague asked her why not she said, "I have too many personal problems." My colleague never saw her again and never did figure out why she came to therapy!

The first step in understanding how therapy works is to understand why people choose to seek help from professionals. Obviously, people come because they have problems that they believe can be helped by treatment. People suffering from depression, panic attacks, painful marriages, divorce, abuse, problems with their children, grief, and hundreds of other problems come seeking the advice and insight of a trained professional to help them understand their difficulties and to get rid of them. But obviously not everyone who has these kinds of problems comes to therapy. Why do some people come for help for these kinds of problems and others stay away? Why do some people who are suffering severely refuse to get help while others who are suffering relatively minor problems come seeking relief?

People come to therapy if they meet four conditions:

1. they are in psychological pain which has recently been intensified by a crisis
2. they have a sense of responsibility that they need to do something about their pain
3. they see the opportunity for help, and
4. they have hope that they can get better.

PAIN

People come to therapy because they are suffering. They are in pain and they believe that their pain has a mental, emotional, or behavioral cause.

Obviously, they don't come to a therapist if they have a sore throat or a broken finger, they come if they have just discovered that their husband is having an affair, they come if they have just spent the past week in bed because they are too depressed to get out of it, and they come because they are too afraid to drive across a bridge they have driven across hundreds of times. Clients come to treatment for thousands of reasons but all of them come because they are in pain. Psychological pain is a necessary condition for treatment.

Psychological pain seems to be one of the driving forces behind human change. Without it no one would make major changes in their lives. Psychological pain comes in many forms: depression, anxiety, fear, anger, frustration, and sadness are perhaps the most frequent. Psychological pain can serve a purpose similar to physical pain: it lets us know that there is something wrong and puts pressure on us to do something to relieve it. If a person has an ulcer, they will not do anything to seek help for it until it starts to hurt. They may seek medical treatment after the pain has persisted for some time. If they do, the physician will prescribe a course of treatment to them and they are likely to follow it initially. However, if the pain is relatively quickly eliminated with the recommended medication, the patient is likely to stop taking the medication before it has finished its work of healing the ulcer. Only when the pain returns are they likely to begin taking the medicine again. They may need to do this several times to prove to themselves that the change they need to make (taking the medication) is important to continue. If the prescribed course of action is right and the patient persists, the ulcer will be healed. The whole process of healing the ulcer is initiated and driven by stomach pain. Without that pain, the ulcer would go undetected, untreated, and may well worsen until the patient begins bleeding and other more serious complications develop. Pain is a message from our internal warning system to make changes until the pain goes away or is at least reduced. Pain is something most of us would like to live without; however, without it we could not live. This seems to be to be true of both physical and psychological pain: we need both to survive.

How, then do such painful emotions as fear, sadness, and anger help us to survive? Aren't they just nuisances to be avoided at all costs? Don't they prevent us from living satisfying lives? I don't believe so. I think psychological pain can guide and spur us to health. Depression, for example, is a very painful mental and emotional state. People who are depressed feel sad, hopeless, guilty, and worthless much of the time. How could such a painful state of mind be helpful? It seems absurd until we look a little more closely. Depression, because it is so painful, is a powerful message to the depressed person that they need to make changes.

They may be helped by anti-depressant medication, but they may also need to make significant changes in their relationships and in the way that they think about themselves and their life. Only by making positive changes will the depression recede and stay away. The pain of the depression can drive them to make these changes, resulting in fuller and more satisfying lives. If they make these kinds of changes, then their depression has been helpful.

Let's look at Nora whom we left entering Dr. Kleinfelter's office for her first therapy session. *Nora was a 53-year-old secretary at an elementary school who had been married to Charlie for over 30 years. They had one child, an 18-year-old son named Quinn who had just recently left home to go to college. She was suffering from some serious and very painful symptoms of anxiety: she was worrying from the time she woke up in the morning until she went to sleep at night. Once or twice a day she would feel particularly panicky and her heart would race, she would feel sweaty, nauseous, and light-headed. These attacks would last about 45 minutes and were terrifying to her. On several occasions, she wondered if she were having a heart attack and considered going to the emergency room for treatment. However, her panic attacks subsided before she left for the hospital.*

Her marriage to Charlie had been very tense the past five years with Nora feeling that he was pulling away from her and wasn't much interested in being close to her. Nora was very close to her son Quinn and worried about him a great deal because he had a rather serious case of asthma. She spent much of her emotional energy making sure that Quinn took his medicine, didn't exercise too strenuously, and ate properly so that he wouldn't have asthma attacks. Despite Nora's worries and her lectures to Quinn, he had begun rebelling against her over the past year by not taking his medication and smoking cigarettes. By doing this, he provoked a rather serious asthma attack and Nora had to rush him to the hospital. He recovered within a few days from the attack, but Nora's worries about her only son intensified greatly. Charlie had been very angry with Quinn for many years for not taking care of himself and often would berate Quinn for his lack of maturity and responsibility. One day, in Nora's presence, Charlie lit into his son for being "stupid", "crazy", and a "complete jerk". He yelled at Quinn for causing his mother to be so upset and told him that he would never "amount to anything". Nora was furious with Charlie for being so cruel to Quinn; so furious that she became cold and distant from him for the next three weeks.

When Quinn left for college a few months later, Nora's worries intensified greatly. She could no longer watch over Quinn as intensely as she had by monitoring his medication, his diet, and his exercise. She feared that he would not take care of himself without her being there to remind him of what he needed to do. Not surprisingly, Nora's panic attacks became more frequent and more severe.

She began to consider getting professional help for her problems with anxiety and she got the name of Dr. Kleinfelter from a good friend of hers who had been a client of Dr. K's and spoke very highly of her.

Nora's anxiety was giving her a strong message which she didn't want to hear: that she was very unhappy in her marriage, that she was angry with her husband and that she was holding on too tightly to her son who was not developing the independence he needed to become a man.

In her first sessions with Dr. K., Nora learned some relaxation techniques that helped her to manage her anxiety a bit better. Dr. K. referred her to a psychiatrist for some medication, which she took dutifully. The combination of the relaxation techniques and the medication began to make her anxiety more manageable but did not eliminate it altogether. However, her problems remained: how was she going to cope with her son being 100 miles away and not being able to prevent him from having another, potentially more serious asthma attack? And what was she going to do with her marriage of more than 30 years which had become so distant and painful over the past five years? As her therapy with Dr. K. progressed, Nora focused more on these issues and less on her now more manageable anxiety symptoms.

If Nora had not become so anxious and had not had her panic attacks, she could have had other symptoms which would have been the result of her very difficult life situation: she could have become seriously depressed, she could have begun drinking or using drugs, or she could have raged at her husband, slapped him in the face and then felt terribly guilty. All of these other types of pain may have driven her to seek help and to begin resolving the problems which had contributed to her pain. However, if Nora had experienced no psychological pain, she would not have known her need to make any changes.

CRISIS

Most people have been in pain for some time before they contact a therapist. As a rule, before people seek therapy, they need a crisis to significantly increase their level of pain. The crisis pushes the sufferer or their family members to the point where they feel they must seek help. For Nora, the crisis came when Quinn left for college and she could no longer take care of him. She had been very worried about her son and had even had some frightening panic attacks, but she did not seek help until her pain was heightened by Quinn leaving home. Another crisis had occurred which had intensified her fears: Quinn had endangered his own life with his asthma attack and Charlie had gotten cruelly angry with their son.

We often think of a crisis as being caused by a tragic or painful event such as the discovery of an affair, the loss of a job, the loss by death of a child or spouse, or a child being suspended from school for behavior problems. Often these types of painful events are the ones which heighten people's pain and bring them to seek help.

Sometimes, however, positive events can cause a crisis which intensifies people's pain. Nora's son Quinn went off to college (a positive event) but the changes resulting from it, for example Nora feeling more afraid for Quinn's health, helped to increase her level of pain. A crisis triggered by positive events is not as unusual as it may seem. In the alcoholism treatment field it is widely observed that when a married alcoholic stops drinking and begins a program of recovery (a positive event), their marriage is often thrown into a crisis and one or both spouses seek therapy.

Crises not only increase the level of pain in people's lives, but they can also convince people that their problems will not go away without professional help. Before her crisis, Nora believed that her anxiety problems would go away when her son left for college and she would no longer have to worry about him every day. She believed that she and Charlie could then enjoy their lives more, being free of the day-to-day responsibilities of parenting. It destroyed her belief that her symptoms would go away on their own and her life would be better than before. Her crisis taught her that she feared deeply for her son's health and even his life and that she could no longer tolerate the way her husband was as a parent. Her crises brought her to a point of great fear and a sense that she would never get better without help. Her crises brought her to Dr. Kleinfelter's office.

RESPONSIBILITY

Nora would not have gone to see a therapist just because she had been in pain for some time and her pain had been increased by a crisis. There are many people who live with a great deal of psychological pain and whose lives seem to stumble from one crisis to another but who never seek help (or do so only half-heartedly to appease someone who suggests it). They may go from one painful relationship to another, from one unfulfilling job to another, they may complain chronically about one of their children or another, they may suffer from chronic depression which worsens when crises come but they do not seek help. Why not? Why do they not seek help when they are in so much pain for so many years? Why do they not seek help even when their pain is made worse by a crisis?

They do not seek help because they believe that their problems are caused by others. They are not convinced that they are responsible for their problems; rather, they believe that they are the victims of someone else's actions. They believe that their problems would be eliminated if only someone else would change and so they wait for that person to change. They often have a long wait.

Nora had a very strong belief that she was respon-

sible to get help if any change was to occur. She grew up as the oldest daughter in a family with a chronically ill brother, Steve, who had a serious case of asthma which he did not manage well at all.

Nora had a long-suffering and chronically resentful mother who leaned on Nora for emotional support, treating her as a friend and confidant. She often depended on Nora to take care of the younger children because her "nerves" were often "shot". Nora felt both complimented by and resentful of all the responsibility her mother placed on her and the position she held in the family as the good and faithful daughter. She was also resentful of the freedom her friends had to lead their seemingly carefree lives. She was frustrated with the fact that her younger siblings resented her mothering role and teased her cruelly about it. She learned well from her position in her family that she was responsible for the emotional well being of her family. Thus it was natural for Nora, when she found herself chronically anxious about her son and her marriage, to take responsibility for getting help.

Nora's younger brother Cal had very little sense of responsibility for himself and others. Cal grew up resenting Nora's bossiness and self-righteousness and dedicated his life to being different from his sister. Since his sister was mom's good little helper, Cal became dedicated to being "bad". His desire to be "bad" came to the fore when he reached adolescence as he began hanging out with guys who did drugs, wore black leather, and rode motorcycles. He snuck out at night to see his rebel girlfriend and would come in at five in the morning on school nights with hickeys on his neck. His father and mother yelled at him and complained to each other about how irresponsible and "no good" he was. Nora and her mother often worried together at night about what they could do to get Cal to straighten out. They often tried grounding and angry lectures but that only made things worse. Cal grew up believing that to be yourself you have to fight authority because the main purpose of authority figures is to make sure you have no enjoyment in life.

Soon after he turned eighteen, Cal discovered that his girlfriend was pregnant and he became more angry, sullen, and defiant than ever. His drug use increased so that he was soon smoking pot daily and using LSD about once a week. He was furious with his parents and with his sister. He told himself that if they had not been such jerks, this never would have happened. He moved in with his girlfriend but fought with her daily. Nora and her mother pleaded with him to get help for his anger, his drug use, and for his "crazy" relationship with his girlfriend. He defiantly refused. He figured that he had made his life what it was and that no one was going to tell him what to do. He certainly didn't want any "damn shrink" messing with his head. Cal was miserable and in the midst of a crisis but was not ready to seek help. He was not able to see that he was causing or at least contributing to his problems and that if his life were going to get better then he would need help in making changes. Despite his mother and his sister giving him a list of four competent therapists and offering to pay for therapy, Cal did not show up in any "damn shrink's" office.

OPPORTUNITY

In order to seek therapy, people must not only be in pain and have a sense of responsibility but they must also realize that they have the opportunity to get help. People have to believe that there are competent professionals in their geographic area whose services they can afford, they have to believe that they have the time to invest in therapy, and they have to believe that therapists can actually be helpful. People's perception of therapy is heavily dependent on the amount of pain they are in and the degree to which they feel responsible for doing anything to solve their problems. The more pain people feel and the more responsible they feel for doing something about it, the more therapy is seen as affordable, available, and potentially helpful. Because Nora was in a great deal of pain and had a strong sense of responsibility, she found therapy worth the money and time and easily convinced herself that therapy could be helpful to her. Being a well-insured public employee, she could afford therapy but, even if she had had less money and time, she would have found a way to get help. However, if she was in poverty and felt completely overwhelmed by the day-to-day demands of her life and had no access to competent, low-cost therapy, she would have simply lived with her pain.

Her brother Cal did not have enough money for therapy nor did he see himself as having much time for therapy. However, his perceptions were highly colored by his resentment towards his family and his feeling that his problems were not his fault. He believed strongly that therapy was worthless and a waste of time and money. Even with his sister and mother being willing to pay for treatment, he saw it as a waste. Because of the way he felt about himself and his family members, he could not be convinced that therapy was worth the effort. Treatment was not an opportunity for him but a waste of time and money. If Nora and her mother had been able to drag him in to see a therapist, he would have proven to his mother and sister that he was right by getting nothing out of treatment. No matter how skillful the therapist had been in affirming him and engaging him in therapy, he would have come out of his first session saying, "that is the biggest load of crap I've ever heard! I can handle things on my own. I don't need that jerk telling me how to run my life!" He would have proven to himself that therapy was a waste of time. His mother and sister would again be left wringing their hands and futilely worrying about Cal. Nora would see the opportunity to get help even when help would be very difficult to find. Cal would see therapy as pointless even if he were brought to the greatest therapist in the world and someone else would pay his way.

The perception that therapy can be helpful is shaped not only by forces within the family and the individual as in the case of Nora and Cal but it is also shaped by previous experiences with therapy and by cultural beliefs about therapy. Obviously, if someone has had a negative experience with therapy which was unhelpful or even destructive, they are less likely to return to treatment. On the other hand, if someone has felt greatly helped by a previous treatment experience, they are much more likely to return. If a culture or sub-culture has a strong bias against therapy, the members of that culture will not see the opportunity which treatment presents. I think this can be seen most clearly in the generation whose members are now in their sixties and seventies. The culture that shaped them believed strongly in self-sufficiency and "pulling yourself up by your bootstraps". Therapy was not widely available in their formative years and most people viewed it either as a luxury for the very rich or handholding for the very crazy. Because of these beliefs, it is very difficult for people who grew up before about 1950 to see therapy as a resource even if they are in great pain. They tend to believe that seeking therapy is a sign that they are "losing their minds" rather than as a potentially helpful way to solve their problems.

Men and women in our culture tend to view therapy differently; these differences provide another example of cultural forces shaping people's perceptions of treatment. About 60% of therapy clients are female partially because females are "taught" by our culture that seeking help for personal difficulties is natural and acceptable. Men tend to be "taught" that seeking help is a sign of weakness which should be avoided because it makes people too vulnerable. As a result, it is more difficult for men to seek out therapy than women. Obviously, there are plenty of women who are "allergic" to professional help and plenty of men who are very open to it. However, because of our culture's prevailing attitudes, the average woman is more comfortable with therapy than the average man.

HOPE

For people to seek therapy voluntarily, they must not only believe that therapy can be helpful in general, but they must also believe that therapy can help them. People often talk themselves out of coming to therapy by persuading themselves that therapy just won't work for them. Some people even tell themselves that they are not worth the time and effort involved in therapy because they are not really worth working on. They believe that they are hopeless. Those who believe that there is no hope that their problems can be improved do not seek help, at least voluntarily. They are simply resigned to the fact that their life can be no better and they can only retreat into bitterness and self-destruction.

Although Nora was feeling hopeless about her problems when she came to therapy, she did have a sense that she could help herself and that she was worth helping. She believed that with the help of a professional she might be able to bring about the changes that she needed to make in order to feel better. Perhaps because of her early training as the responsible helper in her family, she had a deeply ingrained sense that she could help, even with someone as hopeless as herself. Cal, on the other hand, for all his blustering about therapy being worthless had a deeply held belief that he was hopeless. Underneath his tough posturing was a man who felt very powerless to make himself happy. He often felt doomed to a very painful and dissatisfying life although he would not admit these feelings to anyone. One of the reasons that he did not seek help was because he believed that he was powerless to make his life better and that he was not worth the effort.

If you have read this far in this book, you have some hope for yourself. Your hope may be buried deep within you but without it you are unlikely to turn to the next page. Without hope you would certainly not pursue something as challenging, painful, costly, and potentially helpful as psychotherapy.

Pearl of Wisdom: You will make changes in therapy only if you are motivated to do so. If you are motivated for therapy, it is because you are in significant psychological pain that has been intensified by a crisis in your life and you feel responsible for doing something to make things better. You must also see the opportunity for help and have some hope for yourself.

Corollary Pearl of Wisdom: People who are not motivated for therapy cannot benefit from it. Dragging an unwilling participant into treatment is a waste of time and effort. If someone you care about has a problem but is unwilling to seek help, do not try to force them into therapy, seek help for yourself. You may discover that you are protecting them from their pain and from their responsibility for dealing with it. If you can learn to stop protecting them, they might become motivated to seek help. But there are no guarantees.

Chapter 3

Hoping That Others Will Change
and the Birth of the Therapy Triangle

It might seem obvious that most people who come to therapy are hoping to make changes in themselves. However, I have observed that many people who begin treatment are hoping for a change in someone else. At the outset of treatment, most clients believe that their life would be better if their wife, husband, mother, father, child, friend, or boss were different. Most clients who choose to enter therapy say that they themselves need to make some changes but they have an even stronger underlying belief that other people are the ones who need to make the changes which will make their life better. In Chapter 2, I pointed out that in order for people to come to therapy, they must believe that they are responsible for making changes. Very often they believe that they are responsible for getting other people to change. Their thinking goes something like this: "if I can get _____ to change, then I'll feel much better."

In the extreme, the desire of a client to make someone else change can be ludicrous. I once supervised a case in which a 60-year-old woman came to therapy for help with marital distress. She had been married for nearly forty years to a man who was alcoholic and almost never talked to her. She said she had tried "everything" but couldn't get him to change. In one session that took place around Christmas time, she came in and proudly showed her therapist a ten page, single-spaced document in which she had carefully written out 101 New Year's resolutions for her husband!

Most clients are subtler in their desire to change others. They understand intellectually that they can only change themselves. However, they seem to have a more deeply held belief that their problems are the result of someone else who is in distress or is doing them wrong and that if only that person would change, they would be better.

A depressed woman I will call Colleen came to see me. She knew that she was responsible for making any changes that were going to be made in her life, but she also believed that her husband Bill was the cause of all her problems. She believed that if he would become calmer, less angry, more understanding, and wouldn't drink so much, her depression would be relieved. This belief was at least partially right. If Bill had become more open, more understanding, and sober more often, her depression might well have lifted and her pain would have been substantially reduced, at least for a time.

However, he was not about to make these changes. Still, she worried intensely about how she could get him to be different. The more she worried about him, the more she pleaded with him to be different. The more she pressured him to be different, the more he pulled away from her into his work and his drinking. She came to therapy hoping that she would find a way to make him change.

When she was growing up, both she and her mother had worked hard on Colleen's father to try to make him happy. They worked long and hard on him, but he remained angry, distant, and complaining. For Colleen, her marriage was another act of the same play. What she hoped for in therapy was an end to her suffering by a change in her husband; what she had hoped for as a child was an end to her suffering by a change in her father. Her beliefs and feeling ran very deep within her.

Another client named Phil was even subtler in his underlying desire to change someone else. He was a forty-year-old mill worker who came to therapy feeling very discouraged and tearful. His chief complaint was that his wife of eighteen years had begun to be very cool and distant with him. She had recently entered a training program for computer programmers at the local technical college and had been spending most of her spare time with her female friends. Before she made these changes, Rhonda had been a stay-at-home mother and wife who had discontinued her education and employment after high school when she got married.

Phil had grown up with a strong feeling that his mother did not care much for him because she spent so much time running her beauty salon and when she was home she was very critical towards him. Phil spent a great deal of time alone as a child and was often rather sad and withdrawn. He strongly hoped that his mother would love him but he came to believe more and more that she wouldn't. In high school, he drank heavily and smoked marijuana to relieve his pain and to fit in with his friends. Soon after graduation, he stopped abusing alcohol and marijuana because it was not filling the emotional void he felt.

Several years after graduation from high school, he met Rhonda through some friends and he was almost immediately lifted from the fog of discouragement in which he had lived nearly his whole life. She was very attentive to him, thought he was handsome and good (and told him), and devoted herself to him, making all her decisions on the basis of what would make Phil happy. For quite some time, she was very successful at making him happy. They married and had two children in their first three years together. Phil held a secure, moderately well paying job at a paper mill and Rhonda stayed home with the children.

As the children got older, started school and became more independent from Rhonda, she began to feel that there was more for her in life than what she had. She began to feel more and more distant from Phil because he took her for granted and paid less and less attention to her. He spent more time after work fixing up his racecar to run it in local races. She would greet him coolly when he would come home late. He began to return to his feeling of not being cared about or loved. He became more sullen around Rhonda and she became even cooler towards him. She got a part-time job and began attending classes at the local technical college. She began making more female friends and began to see that she was smart, competent, and like-able. Rhonda and Phil spent more and more time apart and when they were in the same house, they were emotionally distant.

One day Rhonda announced to Phil that she was very unhappy in their marriage and that she was thinking seriously about leaving him. There was no other man involved, she just felt strongly that she would be happier with her own life away from Phil. This was the crisis which sent Phil into an emotionally tail spin; he cried uncontrollably, he had difficulty motivating himself to go to work, and he lost interest in his racecar. He also reluctantly made an appointment with a therapist.

Throughout the first session he cried and said that he could not understand why Rhonda had done this to him. He felt that their problems had hit him "out of the blue". He was very down on himself for spending too much time away from Rhonda and for not paying enough attention to her. Underneath these feelings was a powerful belief that he wanted Rhonda again to be dependent on him, to devote herself to him and to make him happy again as she had when they were first together. At home he would plead with her to spend more time with him, to stay away from her female friends, and to drop out of her training program so they could spend more time together. As therapy progressed, he began to look at his relationship with his mother. She was still distant and critical towards Phil and he was very sensitive to her opinion of him. If she would question his decision to buy a new washer and drier, he would become angry and self-doubting; a cloud of discouragement would darken his life sometimes for weeks at a time. Although he could not say this, he wanted his mother to change and to love him for who he was. Similarly, he wanted Rhonda to change back to what she was and love him without the criticism and coolness which he felt so strongly now. At a very deep and mostly unspoken level, he was in therapy to change both his mother and his wife.

THE THERAPEUTIC ALLIANCE
AND THE THERAPY TRIANGLE

When a client enters treatment, it is natural and necessary for him or her to form a positive emotional connection with the therapist, often called a "therapeutic alliance." A collaborative working relationship between client and therapist is an essential ingredient in therapy. However, the therapeutic alliance exists alongside the much more powerful and long-lasting bonds between the client and his or her family members. When the client is in conflict with an important person in their life and is struggling unsuccessfully to change that person, he or she comes to treatment hoping to form an alliance with the therapist so that they can work together on changing the "other". Thus it is natural for client and professional to form their therapeutic alliance in opposition to the person that the client wishes to change. As we shall see, the "therapy triangle" which forms between the client, the therapist, and the "other" has the potential to promote or prevent change for the client. If therapist and client handle themselves well, the client will work on him- or herself to resolve the conflict with the other and grow stronger and healthier as a result. If client and therapist handle themselves poorly, the triangle can become a two-against-one struggle which will become stuck, resulting in no change for the client. The therapy triangle can be pictured like this:

FIGURE 1

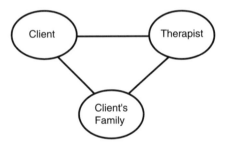

The therapy triangle is an example of an "emotional triangle" which is one of the basic building blocks of human relationships. The more you understand how emotional triangles work, the more you will understand how therapy can be helpful when it works and how it can be unhelpful when it doesn't.

EMOTIONAL TRIANGLES

To understand the therapy triangle, we first need to understand some of the basic principles of all emotional triangles. Emotional triangles (or, simply, "triangles") are present in all human families and organizations. The more a group is driven by fear, the more rigid and powerful are its triangles. Triangles are formed and maintained by fear. They begin when emotional pain such as fear, anxiety, or anger cannot be handled directly by two people who are in a relationship with each other. When the resulting tension between them cannot be resolved, at least one of those people will seek an ally outside of the relationship. The search for an ally outside of the original relationship is usually done naturally and unconsciously; it is not usually a "plot" against the other person in the original relationship. When one person in the original relationship seeks and finds an ally, they get support from their ally and they get relief from the pain in the original relationship at least to some extent and for a while. The "heat" is taken off the original relationship and thus the pain for both members of the original relationship is diffused. However, the difficulties in the original relationship are not resolved because the underlying tension in the original relationship has not changed, it has only been more or less successfully avoided. The pain in the original relationship remains unresolved but more tolerable. The triangle serves both to "stabilize" the original relationship and to make it more difficult to resolve the tension in that relationship. Figure 2 is a diagram showing how emotional triangles work.

FIGURE 2

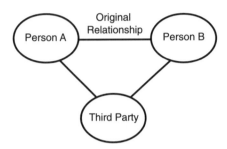

The concept of the emotional triangle is not easy to grasp but I think it will be clearer if we look at some examples. Triangles abound in human relationships and the more you become aware of and think about the principles of emotional triangles, the more of them you will see in your family and elsewhere in your every day life.

KEVIN, MARSHA, AND KEVIN'S WORK

Let's look first at a couple named Kevin and Marsha: Throughout their 10 years of marriage, Kevin and Marsha had become increasing tense with each other. Marsha was afraid that Kevin did not really love her and would one day abandon her either emotionally or physically. Kevin was afraid that if Marsha got too close to him she would control him and he would lose his freedom. Both Kevin and Marsha were afraid of each other but neither was clearly aware of their fear. They both felt a rather vague sense of uneasiness when they were around each other.

Remember, fear is a breeding ground for triangles. Watch how a triangle forms between Kevin, Marsha, and Kevin's work: Kevin is very skilled at his work as a salesman; the harder he works the more he is rewarded financially and personally. As Kevin becomes more fearful of Marsha controlling him and as Marsha becomes more fearful of Kevin abandoning her, Kevin spends more and more time at work. Even when he is at home, he is doing the paper work for his job or is preoccupied with how to sell to his next big account. Marsha senses this and her fear of being abandoned gets worse. As a result, she begins criticizing him about his preoccupation with work. This in turn increases Kevin's fear of being controlled and so he pulls away more from Marsha and involves himself even more in his work. He tells Marsha that he has to work as hard as he does so that she will be able to enjoy the good things that they can buy. Marsha resigns herself to the fact that Kevin will be primarily involved in his work and she just has to live with that.

Kevin is happier being at work where his boss praises him as a bright and rising star than he is at home where Marsha meets him with criticism and quiet, frozen anger. As Kevin pours himself into his work, their relationship becomes much less volatile, and it settles into a distant but tolerable truce. The tension in the original relationship is now tolerable, Kevin has found a great deal of support and nurturance from his job, and Marsha tells herself most of the time that Kevin is working so hard because he has to. The difficulties in the relationship between Kevin and Marsha remain unresolved but their relationship has been stabilized by Kevin's intense relationship with work. If the balance in this triangle is upset, for example by Kevin losing his job, Kevin and Marsha would be faced with each other again and they would experience a very unsettling time until they found someone else with whom they could form a triangle.

GEORGE, STAN, AND THEIR MOTHER

Let's look at another example: the triangle that is formed by a mother, a "good son" and a "bad son". George was the older of two sons and nearly always complied with his parents' wishes. He was an easy baby, a well-behaved, bright, and serious child, and a teenager of whom every parent would be proud.

His younger brother Stan had been a difficult, colicky baby, a mischievous and often irritating child, and a rebellious adolescent. Their mother, June, had always felt closer to George than to Sam. She did have a very strong emotional attachment to Stan as well but that attachment was marked by anger, frustration, and criticism on both sides. She often relied on George for sympathy and comfort when Stan was angry and rebellious towards her. As George grew up, moved out of the house, and got married, his mother continued to depend on him for her emotional support and George struggled to pull away from her, telling her (anxiously but politely) to figure out her own problems. The relationship between June and George became increasingly tense as George struggled to have his own life while trying to make sure his mother was happy.

One way they could temporarily avoid the tension between them was to involve Stan in their relationship. Neither George nor June was aware of the process by which this triangle was formed; it came naturally. Stan frequently got in trouble because he wrote bad checks to cover his gambling debts and would go to his mother for help. She would give him money and then complain to George about how she was always bailing his brother out of messes which Stan himself had created. George would sympathize with his mother and together they would shake their heads about how irresponsible Stan was.

Without being aware of it, Stan "helped" George and his mother by being someone they could always agree on. By focusing on Stan, the struggles between the two of them were avoided and they could get along. Whenever Stan would get in trouble, June would come to his rescue. June and Stan would become intensely involved with each other in their rescuer-victim relationship. This intense involvement between Stan and his mother helped to stabilize the relationship between George and his mother. It "helped" June and her elder son to avoid working out the problems between the two of them. It "helped" George have more freedom from his mother's demands and yet remain close to her. The triangle between June and her two sons kept all three connected to one another in a stable and predictable way but prevented the resolution of the problem between George and his mother. Only when Stan became more responsible, stayed out of trouble for a long time and began to settle down did the original tension between George and his mother resurface. Again, George and his mother could not face the issues between the two of them directly; they began to argue about what George should do with his wife who was depressed. They managed to form another triangle with her.

NORA, CHARLIE, AND QUINN

Let's look at one more example of an emotional triangle before we go on to look at the therapy triangle more closely. In Chapter 1, we met Nora as she was starting therapy with Dr. Kleinfelter. She came to treatment because of an intense and stuck triangle between herself, her husband Charlie, and her 18-year-old son Quinn that had been going on for years.

Nora and her husband Charlie had welcomed

Quinn into the world with great celebration when he was born. Nora and Charlie had been trying to have a child for more than ten years when Nora finally conceived. Both were in their late thirties and had spent many years wondering if they would ever have a child; they were both elated when Quinn was born. Throughout those years, there was a growing dissatisfaction in their marriage as Charlie felt Nora was too preoccupied with having a child and Nora felt Charlie was not supportive enough of her strong desire to become a mother. They did not talk about these feelings because they were both afraid that the other would belittle their feelings. When Quinn turned three, he developed a fairly serious case of asthma which required regular use of an inhaler and a careful eye on his exercise and food intake.

Nora was quick to take nearly all of the responsibility for managing his asthma and became quite over-protective of Quinn. Charlie felt left out of their very tight relationship; he resented Nora because she became preoccupied with her son and had little free time and energy left for Charlie. Charlie also was angry that Nora was "spoiling" Quinn and making him into too much of a "baby". When he felt Nora was being over-protective of Quinn, he would angrily yell at her to let him go. At other times he would take his anger out on Quinn, yelling at him and calling him a "wimp". The more he would yell at Quinn, the more Nora wanted to protect her son and the more Quinn looked to his mother for protection. The more Quinn and his mother were drawn together, the more Charlie's anger burned against both of them. Eventually, Charlie angrily resigned himself to the fact that he could never have the kind of relationship he had wanted with his wife or with his son.

The underlying tension between Charlie and Nora,

which had existed before Quinn was born, was contained in this triangle. Charlie and Nora stayed emotionally involved with each other because of their focus on Quinn; their focus on Quinn made it possible to stay connected but avoid the tension between the two of them. When Quinn left home at eighteen to go to college, Nora and Charlie's relationship became challenged to the point where they had to either resolve the original tension between the two of them or they had to find someone other than Quinn to "triangle in" to their relationship. They tried to do both at once: Nora sought out the help of a therapist.

NORA, CHARLIE, AND DR. KLEINFELTER

As we saw in Chapter 1, the triangle between Charlie, Nora, and Nora's therapist, Dr. Susan Kleinfelter began to form naturally: Nora sought out the help of Dr. Kleinfelter because, after Quinn left for college, she began to have anxiety attacks and she became more discouraged than ever with her marriage. She had felt frustrated with Charlie for many years but with Quinn leaving home those painful feelings had moved to the front of her mind. She also came to therapy because Quinn was doing poorly in college, was not taking care of his asthma appropriately, and was having frequent and dangerous asthma attacks. She worried nearly every waking hour about her only child. Charlie criticized her for worrying so much; she was furious at Charlie for being so callous. When Quinn suffered yet another asthma attack and ended up in the hospital because of it, Nora and Charlie argued bitterly about what they should do with Quinn. Soon after this crisis, Nora called to set up an appointment with Dr. Kleinfelter.

After telling Dr. K this part of her story, Nora began to focus on finding ways to change Charlie so that he would be more sensitive to their son and less angry with her. She talked about how she felt that Charlie needed to resolve things between himself and his bitter and critical mother. She also showed that she was trying to find ways to help Quinn with his asthma so that he would take better care of himself. When she came to Dr. Kleinfelter, she was looking for an ally to help her in the struggle to change her husband and her son.

Dr. Kleinfelter's first reaction was to see Nora as a woman in great distress who had been emotionally abandoned by her husband just when she needed him most. She felt that Nora was a victim and Charlie had some serious problems which needed to be addressed. She saw how much Nora was suffering because of Charlie's callous behavior. When she heard that Charlie was verbally abusive to Quinn, she began to sense the depth of Charlie's problems and the incredible strain that he put Nora under. The therapy triangle was being formed in this very first therapy session. Dr. Kleinfelter was emotionally taking Nora's side against Charlie. Nora was the victim, Charlie was the perpetrator. Nora was fairly healthy and Charlie was "sicker" than his wife. The solution would be for Nora to confront Charlie with his need for help and that if he didn't get help, she would have to leave him. These thoughts were an automatic response for Dr. Kleinfelter and were not clearly articulated in her mind. She had begun to side with Nora against Charlie and a triangle was being born.

Fortunately for both Nora and Dr. Kleinfelter, Dr. K had been well trained to watch out for such emotional side-taking in therapy. She had learned that if she continued to see Nora as a victim and Charlie as a perpetrator that she would not be helpful to Nora. She had enough experience to know that if she continued to "support" Nora in her belief *that Charlie was the root of her problems and that Charlie was the one who needed to change, that Nora would remain stuck in her misery.*

She had seen many clients get entrenched in blaming their spouse or some other family member and either leave them (but continue to blame them) or stay with them (and remain mired in frustration and hurt).

Dr. K was also trained to believe that in relationships there were no "bad guys" and no "good guys"; she knew that each side contributed to the problems, which were presented by people in her office. She knew that if she took Nora's side against Charlie she would only strengthen Nora's belief that she was a helpless victim and make it more difficult for Nora to change. But Nora was unconsciously appealing to Dr. K to join her in the battle to change Charlie. Nora had come to therapy because of her distress, with the belief that it was Charlie who needed to make changes and in the hope that Dr. Kleinfelter would agree with her so that together they could make Charlie see his problems and work on them. Dr. K felt herself drawn to protect and nurture Nora and join her in a crusade to change Charlie. But she knew it wouldn't work. She knew she needed to empathize with Nora in her struggles, she knew she needed to hear and affirm Nora's belief that Charlie was to blame for her struggles, and yet she knew she needed to gently steer Nora toward facing herself and her own contributions to her distress because she knew that only Nora could do something about Nora.

In this vignette, we see Charlie, Nora, and Dr. Kleinfelter beginning to form a therapy triangle. It is forming even though Charlie and Nora are not aware of the process, Dr. K is only vaguely aware of it, and Charlie and Dr. K have not even met! Nora is beginning to feel some relief because someone is listening to her; someone who will take her concerns and worries seriously. She is beginning to feel that she has an ally in her struggle with Charlie. Charlie, on the other hand, is beginning to feel threatened. Nora told him she was going to see Dr. K and he suspects that Nora has been telling Dr. K what a bad husband and father he has been. He fears that Dr. K will put all kinds of ideas of independence into her head and that she will even urge Nora to leave him. He feels fearful and threatened and, as is his style in dealing with fear, he will become critical of Nora and Dr. K and then he will withdraw. Dr. Kleinfelter is feeling drawn to Nora's side because of Nora's neediness and distress. She is beginning to feel some anger towards Charlie and to feel the emotional pull to blame him for Nora's problems. At the same time, she knows she needs to help Nora understand her own role in this drama. Dr. K understands clearly that Nora can only resolve her problems if she stops blaming and trying to change Charlie and begins to work on herself and her own reactions to her husband and her son.

There is a powerful tangle of thoughts, feelings, and relationships involved in this therapy triangle. Whether treatment will be helpful to Nora depends largely on how the three members of the triangle handle themselves. Dr. Kleinfelter has a very difficult task ahead of her as she struggles with her position in this triangle. If she takes sides with Nora against her spouse there will be little or no lasting change for Nora or for Charlie. If she takes Charlie's side or even if she takes a neutral, distant position, Nora may feel abandoned and drop out of therapy.

In our next chapter, we'll take a look at different types of therapists and the roles that they can play in the triangle. We'll also take a look at how Dr. Kleinfelter handled herself in the triangle with Nora and Charlie.

Pearl of Wisdom: If you are like many people, you will go to therapy because of an unresolved struggle with at least one person who is very important to you. You will enter treatment with the hope that someone else will change so that your life will become better. Naturally and perhaps without knowing it, you will form an alliance with your therapist against that other person, thus forming an emotional triangle, the therapy triangle.

Chapter 4

Therapists: The Good, the Bad, and the Overly Helpful

As we have seen, whether your therapy is successful or not depends in good measure on the type of therapy triangle which forms between you, your therapist and your family. The role that your therapist plays in the triangle depends largely on how mature or differentiated your therapist is. The more mature your therapist is, the better chance you will have to resolve your problems and to become more mature yourself.

This chapter is designed to help you recognize a truly helpful therapist: one who will not only help you feel better and get rid of your symptoms but also help you make lasting changes in your life. The techniques used by your therapist are much less important than how your therapist handles the relationship with you in the context of the therapy triangle. If your therapist handles him- or herself well, you will be encouraged, supported and enlightened in dealing with those important others in your life with whom you have painful and unresolved connections. You will have a hopeful sense that you are responsible for learning to connect differently with yourself and with the important others in your life. And you will have a sense that your therapist can help coach you to make the changes you want.

If your therapist handles the therapy triangle poorly, you will stay stuck. Seeing your therapist will serve to increase your level of fear and doubt and will make you less hopeful about making the changes you want to make.

LEVEL OF DIFFERENTIATION

Therapists, like all people, differ in their level of maturity or differentiation. Since mature therapists are so much more effective than their less mature counter parts, it is important that we spend some time understanding what it means to be differentiated.

Dr. Murray Bowen is the theorist most responsible for the concept of differentiation and so we need to look at some of his ideas if we are to understand what makes a good therapist. Dr. Bowen believed that there is a continuum of differentiation (which he represented by a scale from 0 to 100) and that everyone falls somewhere on that continuum. There are not two categories of people: those who are "differentiated" and those who are "undifferentiated"; he believed that people are more or less differentiated.

The essence of differentiation is this: the more mature a person is, the more they are able to be themselves while being closely connected to others. More differentiated people are able to think things through for themselves and not simply react to others. They are able to make choices rather than feel controlled or victimized by others. They have a strong sense that they are responsible for their own lives and therefore spend little energy blaming others or trying to change them. They have a sense of purpose and direction rather than feeling that their life is lived in reaction to others. They have strong convictions and can take strong stands based on those convictions, but they do not try to force others to agree with them. They accept others as they are; they do not spend their energy trying to control them. As I mentioned previously, Dr. Bowen's theory says that all people fall somewhere along a scale of differentiation from 0 to 100, 100 being perfectly differentiated and 0 being not differentiated at all. He writes that very few people are above 70 on the scale; there are no perfectly differentiated people! This can all be summarized in the following diagram:

FIGURE 3

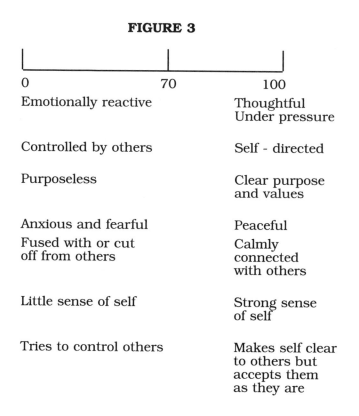

0	70	100
Emotionally reactive		Thoughtful Under pressure
Controlled by others		Self - directed
Purposeless		Clear purpose and values
Anxious and fearful		Peaceful
Fused with or cut off from others		Calmly connected with others
Little sense of self		Strong sense of self
Tries to control others		Makes self clear to others but accepts them as they are

The more a helping professional embodies the characteristics on the right side of the diagram, the more truly helpful they are. The more a professional embodies the characteristics on the left side of the diagram, the less helpful they will be.

I am not saying that a therapist's training, experience, and techniques are irrelevant to their helpfulness; I am simply saying that those qualities are not as important as where they fall on the scale of differentiation. I am also not saying that a therapist's gender, ethnicity, age, or special knowledge about a particular problem are irrelevant to their helpfulness; I am simply saying that their level of differentiation is the most important factor in whether they are helpful or not.

To understand further how mature or immature therapists may conduct therapy, I would like to talk about five types of therapist, four of which are relatively undifferentiated and one of which is relatively differentiated. In this discussion, it is important to remember that these "types" are not distinct categories; therapists cannot be characterized as fitting perfectly into one or another type. Some therapists more closely resemble one "type" of therapist with some clients and more closely resemble another "type" with others. Therapists are as variable as any other group of humans and thus cannot be sorted neatly into airtight compartments. What I am attempting to do is to put a human face on the abstract concept of the differentiation level of therapists.

I will start by discussing the least helpful and fortunately least common type of professional, *the abusive therapist*. I will then describe the types which I think are not as destructive but are not particularly helpful, *the shame-and-blame therapist, the overly helpful therapist, and the withdrawn therapist*. I will end with the type which I feel is most helpful, *the relatively non-anxious therapist*. At the end of each section describing a type of therapist, I will describe how Dr. Kleinfelter would be with her client Nora if she were that type of therapist. I will conclude the chapter by delving into the thoughts and feelings of Dr.

Susan Kleinfelter as she "is": a (relatively) non-anxious therapist struggling to take a (relatively) differentiated stance with her new client.

THE ABUSIVE THERAPIST

Shamefully, there are significant numbers of therapists who abuse their clients. Although it appears that less than 5% of all therapists have abused one or more of their clients, the number is still substantial enough that clients should be forewarned. By "abusive therapists" I mean those professionals who manipulate clients to satisfy their own needs for power and self-gratification in ways which take advantage of the vulnerability of the client and serve to leave the client worse off than when they entered therapy. Such therapists often manipulate their clients into sexual intimacies, they may verbally and physically abuse their clients, and they may control their clients using psychiatric medication.

They can even use mind control strategies similar to those used by extreme religious cults: telling their clients that they are extremely valuable, special, and somehow "chosen" (including sexually seductive remarks and behavior) and at other times telling them they are worthless, horrible, and weak people who can only hope to get better with the help of that particular therapist. The leaders of religious cults often exalt their followers as the chosen few but also abuse them verbally, sexually, or physically for any transgressions of the leader's will and preach to them that salvation can come only by following the leader's divinely inspired teachings. They also drive psychological wedges between their followers and the families of their followers. The more alienated the follower is from their own family, the more power the cult leader has over them.

Relationships between abusive therapists and their clients follow the same pattern. Abusive therapists create an intense bond of dependency between themselves and the client from which the client has a very hard time breaking free. Often, clients are so dependent on their controlling therapist that they cannot see how hurtful "therapy" is to themselves. Long-term clients of abusive therapists become brainwashed in the same way that followers of religious cults do: they cannot see clearly what is happening to them and they have a great deal of difficulty seeing the leader as anything other than a god. Abusive therapists are most often very blaming and critical towards their clients' families and often pressure their clients to have nothing to do with their families. In this type of relationship, the therapist is able to exert great power over the client to gratify his or her own need for power. These professionals work towards destroying their clients' free will and decreasing their client's confidence in their own abilities to help themselves.

Any therapist who is sexually involved with a client is an abusive therapist. So is any therapist who verbally abuses or hits a client. Any therapist who uses psychiatric medication to control and manipulate a client's state of mind so that they will be more susceptible to the directives of the therapist, is an abusive therapist.

My belief is that those clients who are most susceptible to being involved in an abusive relationship with a therapist are clients who have been previously abused in their lives, particularly in their families. The bond between an abusive therapist and a client on the one hand and an abusive parent or spouse and their victim on the other are strikingly similar. Parents who develop an abusive relationship with their children exercise power and control over that child and violate the child's need for safety, freedom, respect, and the need for control over their sexual lives. Children who are chronically abused by parents live in fear of those parents and often feel that they must do exactly what that parent requires so as to prevent their wrath and the abuse which comes with it. These children do not feel that they have the right to their own opinions, feelings, or decisions. They are manipulated by their parents to satisfy the need of their parents for control, not to meet the needs of the child. They are afraid of and dependent upon the abusive parent. Clients who are abused by their therapists feel afraid of and dependent upon their therapists.

Spouses or domestic partners who abuse create a very similar fearful dependence on the part of their victims. They also isolate their victims from possible supportive others, creating a triangle in which the victim is highly dependent upon the perpetrator.

If you were abused by your parents or other family members, you are most likely alienated from and dependent upon your perpetrators. The abusive therapist can exploit this alienation and drive you further from your parents, pressuring you to become more dependent on the therapist. It seems clear that if you had a chronically abusive relationship with a parent or with a partner, you are at some risk to develop an abusive relationship with a therapist.

This of course does not mean that if you enter therapy that you will necessarily develop an abusive relationship with a therapist. It only means that you are used to being hurt and controlled by those in authority and so an unscrupulous therapist may be able to manipulate you without you realizing what is happening. If you are aware that you are at risk for an abusive relationship with a therapist, you may well be able to avoid it by watching out for the following signs of an emerging abusive relationship:

1. You feel your therapist is sexually interested in you.

2. Your therapist tells you that you are very special (more than his or her other clients) and makes special arrangements such as seeing you outside of regular hours.

3. Your therapist disrespectfully puts you down and criticizes you for failure to follow the therapist's plan for you.

4. Your therapist says or implies that he or she is the only person who can help you and that you have to follow his or her instructions exactly to get better.

5. Your therapist uses drugs on you which bring about an hypnotic or unconscious state so as to find out more about your past memories or to understand what may be blocking you from progress in therapy.

If any of these things occur in therapy, you may be headed towards or involved in an abusive relationship. My advice: terminate the relationship immediately, make a complaint to the relevant licensing or law enforcement bodies, and find a therapist who can help you.

If you look back at the diagram of the Scale of Differentiation (page 59) you can see how clearly abusive therapists embody some of the characteristics of relatively undifferentiated people and more subtly embody others. They clearly show an intense need to control others, particularly their clients. They are also very "emotionally reactive" even though most of the time they may appear calm and in control. They can react strongly with anger and fear or with an intensified effort to control and manipulate the client when they sense that the client is exercising some independence from them. Although these therapists appear to be in control of their clients, they are in a sense controlled by their clients because their reactions are greatly dependent on the actions of the client. If the client is compliant with their plans and goes along with the abuse in the relationship, then they are satisfied. If, however, the client objects to the abuse, does not submit to orders, and shows any independence from the therapist, then the professional will react in anger and increase his or her efforts to control the client. By their extreme need to control and degrade the client they become controlled by the client's reactions: they lose their selves in the relationship. They, like most dictators, become dependent on the compliance of their subjects.

Dr. Kleinfelter as an abusive therapist: To understand what an abusive therapist might be like to encounter in therapy, let's imagine how Dr. Susan Kleinfelter might have conducted herself with Nora if Dr. K were such a therapist. When Nora came in for the first session, Dr. K would have worked hard to convince Nora that she was in a very dangerous situation with a potentially explosive man and that she probably had a childhood filled with physical and sexual abuse. When Nora would object that she had no recollection of any such abuse, Dr. K would have insisted (incorrectly) that most people who have anxiety attacks have been severely abused as children but have repressed the memories of that abuse. In order to get well, they must have long-term, intensive therapy to uncover those memories. Dr. K would tell Nora that she was an expert in this type of therapy. Nora would be frightened into returning to see Dr. K: frightened that she would never get better unless she worked with Dr. K for a long time and did exactly what Dr. K said.

Therapy might then consist of Dr. K. pressuring Nora to "remember" things that never happened in sessions involving hypnosis and hypnosis-inducing drugs such as sodium pentothal, the so called "truth serum". Dr. K. would berate Nora when she resisted her therapeutic directives.

Dr. K might also express her sexual attraction for Nora and try to manipulate Nora into a position where they would become sexually involved. Dr. K might require Nora to take many medications and the client's mind would be so clouded that she would feel unable to think for herself. Nora would feel more and more alienated from her husband, her son, and her extended family; Dr. K would tell her in many different ways that her family was the enemy and that only her therapist could help her. Charlie and Quinn would watch as their wife and mother's condition would deteriorate and she became more and more obsessed with and controlled by Dr. K.

This rather bizarre and extreme scenario is fortunately rare but it does happen. There are abusive therapists in practice who behave as Dr. K did in this scenario and there are clients who get hooked into such a relationship. Please be careful out there!

THE SHAME-AND-BLAME THERAPIST

Having become acquainted with the abusive therapist, we are now in a position to understand a type of therapist who is a milder and probably more common version of the abusive therapist: the "shame-and-blame" therapist. These therapists are not abusive in the sense of having sex with their clients, verbally degrading their clients, or physically harming their clients. However, they are very dedicated to controlling their clients. Their "therapeutic" relationships have many of the same patterns as those of their abusive colleagues, but their tactics are less extreme. They believe that by shaming a client when that client does not do what the therapist wants and by blaming the client and the client's family for any lack of progress, the client will comply with what the therapist orders and then the client will get "well". They believe that they know what is best for the client and they preach to their clients that they must do what they say if they want to get well.

Therapists who treat clients this way may have many different theories and techniques that they think are helpful to clients. They may be "family systems" therapists who insist that a client who has unresolved problems with their mother and must confront their mother right away or face the prospect of never getting better. They may be therapists influenced by the writings on domestic violence who insist that their client leave their abusive husband now. They may be Freudian analysts who insist that the only way for a client to improve is to come to therapy three times per week, deal with their dreams and must not leave therapy until their therapist has given them permission. They may be cognitive therapists who insist that the client writes down their negative automatic thoughts and work on changing those thoughts or they will never get better.

The main characteristics of the shame and blame therapist are control and rigidity. Their way is the right way, there is no other, and the client must do what they say if the client is to improve.

Not only will this type of therapist blame the client and try to shame him or her into making changes but they will also blame the client's family members for the client's problems, setting up a very unhelpful therapy triangle. They may think of the client as a helpless victim of their parents, their spouse, or even their children and may strongly take the side of the client against the family. This leads the shame and blame therapist to put pressure on the client to have nothing to do with the family members who the therapist thinks is causing or has caused the client's problems. The therapist may pressure the client to confront those family members with their misdeeds and to have nothing to do with them if their family members don't "get help". Because the client is emotionally attached to these important family members, the client is caught in a bind between obeying the directives of the therapist and thus cutting off from their family members, or disobeying the directives of the therapist and thus risking the blame of the therapist. If you refer back to the discussion of the therapy triangle in Chapter 3, you will see how the shame-and-blame therapist helps to keep the triangle stuck and actually prevents genuine change from taking place in the client.

The type of relationship which the shame-and-blame therapist tends to set up with their clients is like the attachment between a very controlling, critical parent and their dutiful but resentful child. In that type of parent-child relationship, the parent always knows what is best for the child (even when the "child" may be 40 years old!).

The parent tells the child what to do, and if he or she fails to do that, uses shame and guilt to try to control the child into doing what is "right" and "for the child's own good". The child then has the choice of obeying the parent's demands and thus thwarting their own needs or disobeying their parent and thus risking being blamed and unsupported by the parent for "rebelling" against them. With these choices, the child has a very difficult time developing a secure and independent sense of self, separating from their parent, and becoming a mature adult.

Similarly, the shame and blame therapist tries to control the client into getting better. They praise the client for doing what they have told the client is the right thing to do and they blame the client for not doing the right thing. This does not lead to growth on the client's part; rather, it leads to a resentful dependence on the therapist. The client tries to comply with the therapist (because, after all, the therapist knows best) and yet feels stifled and frustrated. The client certainly does not improve their ability to deal with their own problems because they are punished for doing so. They are so busy either complying with or resisting the therapist that they don't learn to think for themselves. Real and lasting change in their presenting problems becomes impossible because they cannot move towards a higher level of differentiation.

If we look back again at the scale of differentiation (page 59) we can see how the shame and blame therapist has strong characteristics of the relatively undifferentiated individual. Like the abusive therapist, they focus on controlling their clients into health. They are very emotionally reactive and fearful when their clients deviate from their narrowly defined therapeutic path. Not only do they use fear to motivate their clients, they themselves are motivated by fear: the fear that their clients will not comply and thus will not improve. They also tend to "fuse" with their clients in the sense of developing a tight, often smothering bond with them in their attempts to help their clients. They become overly invested in whether their clients improve or not and have a great deal of difficulty letting their clients find their own way. They are often scolding towards their clients for leaving therapy before they are done and warn them of the dire consequences of not continuing in therapy. This type of therapy is often good for the therapist's bank account because, if they are skillful, they can control clients into continuing in therapy for a long period of time. This type of therapy can also shore up the professional's sense of superiority and self-righteousness. The sense of self-righteousness possessed by the shame-and-blame therapist can be a way of compensating for his or her own high levels of fear and self-doubt.

As we saw earlier with the abusive therapist, it seems natural that individuals who have been abused, controlled, and blamed by their parents or significant others and who have tried to comply with the demands of those others stand the best chance to develop and maintain a relationship with a shame-and-blame therapist. Although anyone can see a therapist of this type for a few sessions, people who have a pattern of being put down by family members would tend to continue in a relationship with a professional who would tell them exactly what they needed to do and demand that they do it. When the therapist would tell them exactly what they should do, the client would then try hard to comply in order to please the therapist. When they deviated from the therapist's plan, they would blame themselves for doing so, and try harder next time to be "good". They might resent the therapist's control over their lives but feel compelled to obey the therapist. They would be in a relationship pattern which they learned in their family; therapy would feel like home. It would be most unlikely for them to make significant or lasting changes in treatment

If you are susceptible to this kind of relationship in therapy because you have experienced it with a parent, spouse, or other significant person in your life, you might need to watch carefully for the following signs that you have found a shame-and-blame therapist:

1. Your therapist in the first few sessions begins insisting that you must take certain courses of action (such as breaking off a significant relationship) if you ever hope to get better.

2. When you try something which the therapist suggests and it doesn't work, your therapist blames you and says (perhaps in sophisticated clinical terminology), "I told you so".

3. Your therapist insists that you attend certain seminars or classes, insists that you join certain therapy or support groups, or insists that you read certain books and states that without doing these things you will never get better.

4. When you don't do what your therapist has insisted that you do, he or she threatens to not see you in therapy anymore unless you comply.

5. Your therapist tries to make you do certain things about which you feel very uncomfortable. You

express your discomfort and reluctance and he or she ignores or rides roughshod over your discomfort, continuing to insist that you do what he or she wants.

If you have a history of being in a relationship with a controlling and blaming person and you are at a particularly vulnerable time in your life (which is true of most therapy clients) then you are at risk to bond firmly with a shame-and-blame therapist. You may see some brief improvement in your problem as long as you comply with your therapist's wishes but you will not grow as a person nor see long-lasting improvement. My advice: end the relationship and find a more flexible, accepting therapist who will guide you rather than coerce you.

Dr. Kleinfelter as a shame and blame therapist: If Dr. K were a shame-and-blame therapist, she might tell Nora in the first or second session that her husband was the root of all her problems and that she should move towards divorce as soon as possible. When Nora would balk at this (as she naturally would) Dr. K would pressure her even harder to do so, telling her that she would never get better unless she got rid of Charlie. She might label Charlie a "rage-oholic" and tell Nora that he must get help or there would be no hope for their marriage. When Nora would defend Charlie and point out to her therapist that Charlie was not as bad as Dr. K believed, she would be accused of being "in denial" and unable to know what is best for her. She might be told that she must attend a group for battered spouses and that she must see Dr. K weekly for the next year in order to have any chance of getting better.

In subsequent sessions, Dr. K would pressure Nora

to leave Charlie and at times threaten to stop seeing her in therapy if she was going to resist therapy by refusing to do what Dr. K told her to do. Over time, Nora would become less confident in her own abilities to solve her problems and more dependent on Dr. K's directives. She might alternate between angrily blaming Charlie and feeling very dependent on him. She would blame herself as "a bitch" for her angry tirades towards him and she would blame herself for being so weak that she needed him so much. She would be confused, self-doubting, and worse off than when she first came to see Dr. K.

THE OVERLY HELPFUL THERAPIST

Some therapists believe that they can be so loving and nurturing to a client that they can make them healthier by the power of their love. Their implicit message to the client is "I will love you into getting better, I will nurse you to health." The late Virginia Satir, a world-renown family therapist, once said that when she began her professional career she felt as if her whole body were covered with breasts with which she could nurse and nourish her clients. It does appear to be true that in any successful treatment, it is essential for the therapist to care about the client and to be able to communicate that caring to him or her. However, the overly helpful therapist believes that the curative force in therapy is his or her ability to nurture the client, not the client's ability to make changes in him- or herself.

The overly helpful therapist readily praises and affirms clients when they are working towards making changes that the therapist believes are "healthy". However, when the client takes a step with which the therapist does not agree (such as getting involved in an "unhealthy" relationship), the therapist becomes anxious and feels that he or she has failed to be helpful enough. When the client gets stuck, relapses, or takes an action which the therapist believes is "unhealthy", the overly helpful therapist tends to blame him- or herself for the problem and becomes nervous and controlling with the client. The therapist may begin to anxiously warn the client about the dangers that lie ahead and to subtly try to control the client into more "healthy" behavior. The client may begin to resent the therapist and either want to rebel by pursuing a course of action of which their therapist does not approve, or submit to what the therapist says (to relieve the anxiety of the therapist!). Either way, both client and therapist get confused as the client reacts to the professional's fear that he or she is somehow failing to be helpful enough. Under these circumstances, the client has difficulty learning to take responsibility for his or her life because he or she is either trying to prove that the therapist is wrong or trying to please the therapist so that the therapist will feel better. Within this type of treatment relationship, the client has a hard time "growing up".

The type of bond that is often established between the overly helpful therapist and his or her clients is similar to the relationship between an over-protective parent and his or her children. These types of parents are extremely attentive to their children's needs, are filled with doubts about their own abilities to meet those needs, and are anxious about their child's ability to cope with the difficulties of life. These types of parents can be very affirming and nurturing to their children but have a great deal of difficulty encouraging their children to develop enough independence to function well in a challenging world. If they are not too fearful about their children and about their own abilities to parent, they can be excellent parents of young children but have increasing difficulty as their children grow older and develop more autonomy. As their children grow up and begin to disagree with and disobey their parents, these types of parents begin to doubt their own parenting abilities and anxiously attempt to control their children into acting, feeling, and thinking the way the parents think they should. This leads the children into either rebelling or complying.

Similarly, the overly helpful therapist, if he or she is not too anxious, can be very helpful to some clients particularly in the early stages of therapy when the client is often vulnerable, confused, and filled with self doubt. The nurturance of the therapist can help them to gain confidence in themselves and begin to take the steps they need to improve their lives. However, as the client gains in confidence and independence, the overly helpful therapist may become threatened and may work (unconsciously, usually) to get the client back to being dependent. When this happens, both therapist and client are likely to get stuck either in an anxious parent/rebellious child pattern or in an anxious parent/compliant child pattern. In either case, the client remains a child and has difficulty growing towards adulthood.

If we look again at the Scale of Differentiation diagram on page 59, we can get an idea of how an overly helpful therapist embodies the characteristics of a relatively undifferentiated person. As we have seen, the overly helpful therapist can be quite emotionally reactive to his or her clients. In fact, their emotions tend to be controlled by the client: if the client is making progress, they feel calm but if the client relapses, makes a wrong turn, or is slow to change, they feel very uneasy. These therapists doubt that they are helpful enough and they doubt that their clients are strong enough to help themselves. Their sense of self is somewhat shaky particularly when their ability to nurture does not produce the expected improvement in the client. They tend to develop relationships with clients in which they are too dependent on how the client does in therapy for either client or therapist to be emotionally free in the relationship.

They usually see themselves as non-controlling towards their clients and believe that their nurturance is "unconditional", that is, not dependent upon whether the client improves or not. However, as we have seen, they are prone to become controlling when the client feels, thinks, or does something which the therapist thinks is unhealthy. At that point, they try to control the client into health.

Many clients are drawn initially to an overly helpful therapist, particularly if that therapist is not too extreme in their need to be helpful. The overly helpful therapist, as I have pointed out, can be quite nurturing to the client who is very distressed. Of course, most clients entering treatment are in a very painful crisis and they feel burdened with the responsibility to make things better for themselves and those around them (see Chapter 2). They are confused about what to do next and they doubt their own abilities to help themselves. It makes sense that they would respond well to the nurturance of the overly helpful therapist and make significant gains early in therapy. However, as the client matures and grows in confidence, they may not make as much progress with the overly helpful therapist.

They may stick with this type of therapist for some time because the therapist was so caring and helpful to them in a very difficult point in their life, but they may find it more and more difficult to make progress. They may have a vague sense that the therapist is trying to control them or they may be downright resentful of the therapist.

They may feel unchallenged by the therapist because the therapist is working too hard to get the client to like them. Furthermore, they may feel that the therapist has taken their side too much against the significant others in their lives, and has spent too much energy blaming the client's spouse, parents, or children for the problems which the client is experiencing. As we saw previously, in this situation, the therapy triangle tends to get stuck and the client's progress stops. Often the clients of overly helpful therapists leave therapy feeling somewhat better about themselves and with their problems somewhat resolved but without having developed a clear direction for how to help themselves with future challenges. They may find themselves in another crisis in the near future and seek out therapy once again.

To summarize, here are some signs which indicate that you may have found an overly helpful therapist:

1. Your therapist is very supportive and nurturing to you particularly at the beginning of the relationship but tends to pity you, see you as incapable of helping yourself, and sees you as the victim of others' actions.

2. When you report to your therapist that you have taken an action or made a decision that your therapist does not think is "appropriate" or "healthy", he or she becomes anxious and tries to be even more helpful and nurturing but may in the process become quite controlling.

3. You have a sense that your therapist is working too hard for you to like him or her and is working too hard to get you to "improve" (as defined by the therapist).

If you feel you are working with an overly helpful therapist who is not extreme in their need to help, my advice would be to stick with that therapist until you feel that you are no longer being helped. You are likely to feel better about yourself early on in therapy and make some progress in your ability to cope with, control, or eliminate the problems which you brought to therapy. However, you may come to feel controlled by your therapist, overly close to your therapist, or begin to sense that your therapist is taking your side against your family members. When you begin to experience these kinds of thoughts and feelings, my advice would be to listen to and trust them, perhaps talk to your therapist about them, but if they persist, find a therapist who does not need you to change so much and who can help you move closer to your goals.

Dr. Kleinfelter as an overly helpful therapist: Dr. K would be very supportive of Nora in her pain and would give Nora a great deal of positive feedback during the initial session. She would tell Nora that it must be very painful and discouraging to have to struggle so hard in her marriage and with her son. She would emphasize the difficulties and pain that Nora was going through but she would also imply that Nora was a victim of her husband and her son. She might label Charlie's anger as "unhealthy" and Quinn's behavior as "immature". She might be a bit too gushy in her support of Nora. Nora might feel better after a few sessions: less self-blaming and more confident in her ability to solve her problems. She might begin being more assertive with Charlie and try harder not to shrink from conflict with him. She might also begin setting firmer limits with Quinn and not catering to his every need, letting him solve his own problems, and allowing him more independence. She would find herself being more assertive with both her husband and her son but also being more blaming and more strident. When they failed to change as she hoped, she would become discouraged and would go to Dr. K for support. Her overly helpful therapist would readily give Nora that support along with messages that Charlie and Quinn were really unhealthy and that she should "confront" them more forcefully, trying to get them to change. Nora would try again, with limited results.

Dr. K might suggest that Nora bring her husband and or her son into joint counseling sessions but Charlie and Quinn would soon get the sense that Dr. K was on Nora's side and would pull away from therapy. Nora would become more and more frustrated and Dr. K would as well. Dr. K would begin to doubt her own competence as a therapist and begin to doubt Nora's commitment to change. She would tend to blame herself or to blame Nora. The two of them would remain stuck for some time in therapy without significant, long-lasting progress.

THE WITHDRAWN THERAPIST

The withdrawn therapist is often the therapist who is caricatured in the popular media. He or she says virtually nothing throughout the therapy session as the patient, at times lying on a couch and not facing the therapist, relates their dreams, their fantasies, and their feelings. The therapist may take notes during the session but says nothing or almost nothing until the end of the session when he or she says, "let's pick this up at our next session". The client dutifully returns to many of these sessions and is often no more clear at the end of therapy how to deal with their problems than they were when they came in. The withdrawn therapist is quite reluctant to explain to the client what they think is causing the client's problems, preferring that the client discover this for themselves. The therapist is extremely reluctant to reveal anything about him- or herself to the client and often is rather cool and humorless in their relationship to the client. The withdrawn therapist holds him or herself stiffly aloof from the client, seemingly afraid that any warmth, advice, or emotional engagement on the part of the therapist will distort the process of therapy and make it more difficult for the client to understand him- or herself.

Clients often feel confused and abandoned in therapy with this type of therapist. They feel that their therapist does not really care about their problems nor can he or she explain to them why they are struggling with those problems. They get very frustrated because they keep talking about similar things in every session, but do not learn anything about themselves nor do they figure out what they need to do to get better. Many clients drop out of this type of therapy because they do not see any results and because it is often quite expensive. The therapist may tell the client that they are quite disturbed and they need to keep coming back several times a week for years if they hope to get better. The client feels guilty if they leave therapy but feel they are not getting anything out of it. The client keeps hoping for a breakthrough but it rarely comes. Occasionally it may come when the client realizes that the therapy is not doing them any good and then exercises the independence necessary to drop out. The client may have improved a bit in their ability to make independent decisions without the approval of their parents.

The bond between the withdrawn therapist and their clients (particularly if those clients stay in therapy for an extended period of time) is similar to the relationship between a cool, aloof, and emotionally distant parent and a rather fearful and compliant child. The parent is not particularly clear about what the child is to do to please the parent but is rather stern and critical when the child misbehaves. The child wants very strongly to be loved and cared for by the parent but the parent stays aloof, afraid of getting too close. The child remains confused what he or she needs to do to please the parents and this serves only to strengthen the child's resolve to be a "good". It also serves to increase the level of the child's anxiety and fear as he or she very carefully monitors his or her own behavior hoping for a scrap of affection from the parent. The child has a great deal of difficulty growing up and becoming truly and freely themselves because they continue to try to focus on pleasing their parent rather than feeling free to be themselves. They may seek out others upon whom they can be dependent (such as a spouse) or they may desperately seek nurturance in ways which will ultimately be unrewarding such as alcohol and other drugs, promiscuity, or workaholism.

The withdrawn therapist clearly exemplifies one of the characteristics of relatively undifferentiated individuals: the tendency to "cut off" from others as a way of dealing with difficulties in relationships. When a relationship becomes too emotionally charged, the person distances him- or herself from the other because they fear that painful things will happen if they get too close. You can observe this in extreme form in relationships between siblings who have not spoken to each other in 10 years or in adult children who have not seen their parents in five years and then at a wedding or funeral they engage in five or ten minutes of superficial (but emotionally charged!) chat. Usually cut offs are done because one or both people involved fear that if there is any closeness, painful things will happen such as anger outbursts, unwanted sexual relationships, betrayal, or criticism. Cut-offs are done because people fear involvement, not because they don't care.

It may be that withdrawn therapists hold themselves so aloof from their clients because they are afraid that there will be too much involvement if they let their guard down. They are afraid that any emotional involvement between therapist and client will distort and taint the process of therapy. To my way of thinking, therapy cannot begin unless there is some emotional engagement between therapist and client. Clients who work with withdrawn therapists often report that they got very little out of treatment.

You might watch out for the following signs that you have been seeing a withdrawn therapist:

1. You have seen the therapist for at least three sessions and you have no more idea what is causing your difficulties or what to do about them than you did before. This is usually because the therapist has not said what he or she thinks about your problem.

2. Your therapist is aloof, remote, and conveys a sense of superiority to you.

3. Your therapist seems more interested in getting

you hooked into therapy on a frequent and regular basis than he or she does in helping you understand and solve your problems.

4. Your therapist nearly always responds to a direct question about what he or she thinks about your problems with "what do you think?" or a similar remark which deflects the question back to you and leaves you as confused as you were before.

My advice if you are seeing a withdrawn therapist: find another therapist because they won't be worth your time, money, and energy.

Dr. Kleinfelter as a withdrawn therapist: Nora would describe her problem to Dr. K. and Dr. K would listen thoughtfully, saying little. In fact the entire first session might pass with Dr. K. saying little more than "uh-huh", "can you tell me more?", and other such comments. At the end of the session, Dr. K would set Nora up for a series of appointments, perhaps more than one per week and Nora would leave. The next session would be much the same although it is possible that Dr. K would steer the sessions towards Nora talking about her dreams and fantasies, rather than what is currently going on in her life. She would get little or no feedback from Dr. K on what Dr. K thought the problem was and how therapy would help Nora. Dr. K might give an explanation to Nora but it would be very difficult for Nora to understand and would seem to have little relevance. She would continue with months of such sessions without understanding any more about herself and with no idea about what to do to solve her problems. She would either drop out in frustration or keep going largely because Dr. K would tell her that she must be in long-term, intensive (i.e. frequent) therapy in order to get better.

THE (RELATIVELY) NON-ANXIOUS THERAPIST

The most helpful therapists are those who embody most closely those characteristics of the relatively differentiated person which are listed on the right side of the diagram on page 59: They are thoughtful rather than reactive, they are self-directed rather than controlled by others, they are clear about their own purpose and values without pushing their values on others, they have inner peace rather than high levels of anxiety, they can connect emotionally with others without becoming fused with them or having to cut off from them, they have a strong sense of themselves, and they can easily allow others to be themselves. There are no perfectly differentiated people therefore there are no perfect therapists. My purpose in this section is to describe therapists who are relatively differentiated and relatively non-anxious because these are the therapists who are going to be most helpful to you. I want to describe the relatively non-anxious therapist so that you can recognize him or her in your therapeutic endeavors and, by doing so, get the most benefit you can from treatment.

The relatively non-anxious therapist can emotionally connect with clients so that a collaborative alliance is formed between therapist and client. The therapist can give emotional support, affirmation, advice, and explanations of the client's thoughts and feelings without trying to pressure the client to accept any of what the therapist offers. This type of therapist listens very well to the client and can communicate to the client in language which they can understand and about issues which the client is interested. They also clearly communicate that what the client does with the therapist's interpretations and advice is up to the client. They are very clear that they are not trying to control the client. Clients or relatively non-anxious therapists most of the time feel understood, respected, and challenged to work on themselves.

To put it another way, the relatively non-anxious therapist is able to care about, respect, understand, and even enjoy their clients without needing them to get better. This is difficult for therapists to do because their reputations and professional self-esteem are based largely on whether or not significant numbers of their clients get better through working with them. However, if they feel that their clients must get better by working with them, they end up controlling them and their clients are not helped in the long run. In the descriptions of the abusive therapist, the shame-and-blame therapist, the overly helpful therapist, and the withdrawn therapist, there is one characteristic which is true of all of them: they ultimately seek to control their clients into getting better. However, the relatively non-anxious therapist can let their clients alone enough so that the client can change or not change as they wish, not as the therapist wishes. As a result, this type of therapist avoids rescuing his or her clients and yet does not abandon them.

The relatively non-anxious therapist collaborates with their clients without smothering them. He or she allows their clients to feel their emotional pain and is able to support and guide them through it without rescuing them from it. Alleviating the client's pain is ultimately the client's job. In the context of a relationship like this, the client learns to work on whatever they need to in order to heal rather than depending on the therapist to magically take their pain away from them.

The relatively non-anxious therapist also handles blame differently than the therapists that were described in the previous sections. They tend to blame neither the client nor the client's family for the problems which exist. They tend to see the problems in the client's life as no one's fault but as a natural occurrence. It is very difficult for the therapist not to blame the client's parents when the client has been sadistically abused and tortured by them from infancy on. It is very difficult for the therapist not to blame the client when the client gets involved with her eighth abusive boy friend and she cheerfully reports that this boyfriend is "different" and "he'll change". Nevertheless, this type of therapist strives to blame neither client nor the "other" because he or she knows the power of blame to create unhelpful therapy triangles which serve to keep people stuck in painfully repetitive patterns.

The relatively non-anxious therapist is able to remain "thoughtful" with clients rather than reactive to them even in the most difficult circumstances. By this I mean that they do not have an answer for everything and they are actually thinking about the client's dilemma rather than giving the client easy stock answers to their problems. They are willing to say "I don't know" to a client and really mean it. They have a thoughtful air about them which shows they really are concerned about the client and they are not trying to force them to follow a path which is not of the client's own making.

Finally, this type of therapist enjoys doing therapy and even has fun with it. In fact, I believe that therapy is more enjoyable and fun to these therapists than to any others. They are able to take their clients seriously and yet, because they are not ultimately responsible for their clients, they are freer to enjoy them. If therapy is a grimly serious business, and the therapist is responsible for how every one of their clients "turns out", then the therapist will become burned out, unhappy, and resentful of his or her clients (particularly the ones who don't make progress quickly). A warm sense of humor is only possible for a therapist to maintain if that therapist is both caring towards his or her clients and yet not responsible for them. In fact, the relatively non-anxious therapist is responsible to but not responsible for their clients. This attitude enables him or her to stick with therapy as a career without becoming burned out and to stick with difficult clients without losing patience or resorting to blame or control.

To summarize, here are the signs that you have found a (relatively) differentiated therapist:

1. Your therapist consistently does things which help establish a collaborative alliance with you namely, listening carefully to you, respecting your feelings and your point of view, and treating your problems and struggles as important.

2. Your therapist can be supportive and nurturing but does not pressure you to agree or conform to what he or she is saying.

3. Your therapist challenges you to make changes but does not control you into making changes.

4. Your therapist blames neither you nor others in your life for your problems.

5. Your therapist seems to genuinely enjoy doing therapy.

If you happen to find a therapist like the one I have just described, my advice is simple: stay with them. You will make progress with them even if they are not particularly knowledgeable about your specific problem, even if they have less formal education than another therapist might, and even if they are not the same (or a different!) race, gender, age, or ethnic group as you. You have found a helpful therapist and they are not always easy to find.

Dr. Kleinfelter as she is, a (relatively) non-anxious therapist: Back in Chapter 3, we talked about Nora's first session with Dr. Susan Kleinfelter and we noted how a therapy triangle was being born. We also talked about how Dr. Kleinfelter automatically reacted to taking Nora's side against Charlie; she felt herself drawn immediately to the belief that Nora was a victim and Charlie a perpetrator. She felt sympathy for Nora's plight and anger towards Charlie's insensitivity. She was beginning to take sides, to blame, to feel anxious about the outcome of therapy and was wondering how Nora would handle the difficult task of having such an insensitive husband. By reacting to Nora as she did, Dr. K showed us that she is not perfectly non-anxious! She is, however, a relatively non-anxious therapist, so if we look at how she handled her initial sessions with Nora, we will get a sense of how these types of therapists handle themselves.

Dr. K began by asking Nora about Nora's experience of the problem. She listened very carefully not only to understand what was going on currently in Nora's life but also to understand Nora's past and how that might be contributing to her current problems. More important than what Nora and Dr. K talked about was the atmosphere which was created between Nora and Dr. K. It was an atmosphere of respect, thoughtfulness, and collaboration.

Nora felt that Dr. K was listening very carefully to her, not only to what she said but also to the feelings and thoughts behind what she was saying. Nora felt respected and neither judged nor pressured. Furthermore, Nora felt that Dr. K was not taking sides in her struggles with Charlie and with Quinn. Although Dr. K's initial reaction was to side with her against her husband, Dr. K was able to think things through enough to get to a less anxious and less blaming way of thinking and feeling. As a result, Nora felt that Dr. K. respected her husband and her son and did not judge them as "sick" or "dysfunctional".

Nora got the sense that she could be free to tell Dr. K anything without Dr. K jumping to conclusions. She began to see that Dr. K would remain thoughtful and calm but would be involved in working with Nora to solve her problems. Dr. K would help Nora make sense of her feelings, her thoughts, and her problems by gently and respectfully sharing what Dr. K thought was going on with Nora. As their sessions proceeded, Nora felt freer and freer to explore her own thoughts and feelings and felt supportively challenged to work towards her own solutions to the problems which she faced. Dr. K might or might not suggest that Nora bring Charlie and/or Quinn into the sessions but she would probably be open to that if Charlie or Quinn were open to it and, of course, if Nora did. Depending upon Dr. K's approach to therapy, she might focus more on Nora's thoughts, her feelings, her past family relationships, or her current family relationships but she would create the same emotional atmosphere between her and Nora no matter what her approach was.

Nora naturally was dominated by many fears at the beginning of therapy. She was afraid that Dr. K may judge her, that she would look into herself and not like what she would find, that she might decide to make big changes in her life (such as divorcing Charlie), and that she might be really "sick". As we shall see in the following chapters, Nora became less fearful and thus freer to work on devising her own solutions to her problems. We will see how she was challenged by Dr. K. to find her own way through the tangle of thoughts, feelings, behaviors, relationships, and problems which made up her life. We will see how she felt stronger and stronger as therapy went on although at times she felt worse as she faced particularly painful and difficult issues. She felt both supported and challenged by the caring, calm, and wise presence of Dr. Kleinfelter.

Pearl of Wisdom: Therapists are like people; some are more mature and wiser than others. Wise and mature therapists, those who are most "differentiated", are the most helpful therapists, regardless of their area of specialization, their particular theoretical orientation, their gender, their race, or their age. If you have found one, keep working with him or her.

Chapter 5

Differentiation (Part I):
Becoming Yourself While Being With Others

We have come to the point in this book where we need to focus intently on what you, the client, can do to make significant and lasting changes in your life with the help of your therapist. Previous chapters have focused on your motivations for therapy, your hope that others will change, how you might form therapy triangles, and the types of therapists you might encounter. This chapter focuses on what you need to work on if you are to truly benefit from treatment. Remember that therapy is not surgery and cannot be done to you; only through your own efforts to change yourself will you get lasting benefits from treatment.

In Chapter 4, I focused on the idea that the more mature or "differentiated" a therapist is, the more helpful he or she can be. This chapter will focus on the parallel belief that the more mature or "differentiated" you become, the healthier you will be. To become more differentiated requires work on your ability to be your true self while being closely and non-anxiously connected with others. If you can increase your level of differentiation, not only will the problems for which you sought therapy be less troublesome, but you will also be more "immune" to other problems in the future.

DIFFERENTIATION: BECOMING YOURSELF
AND BEING WITH OTHERS

Differentiation is the process of the growth of the self. There are two forces which pull and push on all of us:

a force which pushes us away from others and a force which pulls us towards others. Stated more completely, there is a force which pushes every person to become a separate, independent, and emotionally distinct individual who can "think, feel and act for himself" (Kerr and Bowen, p. 95) and there is a force which propels everyone in any human group or family "to think, feel, and act as one" (same reference). The process of the development of each person's self, or differentiation, is the process of balancing these two forces. Differentiation is the process which, if carried far enough, leads a person to be completely one's own person and yet be able to connect closely with others. As we saw in Chapter 4, no one ever becomes perfectly differentiated so no one is able to be completely him- or herself and yet connect closely with others.

People who are well differentiated are very clear about their purpose and values and thoughtfully shape their life according to their purpose and values.

At the same time, they can maintain close and peaceful relationships with the important people in their lives. The highly differentiated person can listen thoughtfully to individuals who are highly critical of them without losing their focus and without trying to force those other people to have the same values and purpose as themselves. Perhaps some of the great religious leaders of humanity have most closely approached this ideal and might be seen as the only highly differentiated people who have lived on earth.

In order to understand the concept of differentiation more concretely and practically, I would like to present an illustration from the movie "Ordinary People." The movie begins with Calvin (played by Donald Sutherland) and his wife Beth (played by Mary Tyler Moore) attending a play. When the play is over and they are leaving the theater, Calvin anxiously asks Beth, "Well, did we like the play?" In that one question (the first line spoken in the movie by the main characters) the director establishes that this couple is not very well differentiated. This question assumes that both Calvin and Beth must have the same opinion about the play in order to keep the peace between them. Indeed, the rest of the movie bears out what a difficult time this family has in dealing with conflict and differences.

As the movie unfolds, the viewer comes to understand that the family's "traditions" are that every one must agree on all things in order to stay together and if there are any differences, then people must angrily disconnect from each other. They are not able to be their own individual selves and, at the same time, stay securely connected to each other.

If Calvin and Beth were more highly differentiated individuals, their dialogue after the play might have gone like this:

Calvin: How did you like the play?

Beth: Oh, I loved it. It really moved me and made me think about a lot of things in my own life. It was one of the best plays I've seen in years.

Calvin (Surprised that she liked it so well but not threatened by that nor afraid to express his own, very different perspective on the play): You know, to be honest, I didn't get it at all. I was bored during the whole play and almost fell asleep a couple of times. I'm glad you liked it, though.

Beth (Feeling comfortable that she loved the play and he was bored by it): Yeah, I thought it was really great. The scene when the two lovers were quarrelling and the woman's husband was listening to them from behind the wall was just amazingly well done. What was it about the play that bored you?

These people are comfortable with their own feelings and perceptions of the play and are not afraid or threatened by the fact that their partner has a completely different reaction to the play. They don't feel much pressure to change their own feelings and thoughts about the play to conform more closely to their partner's. Nor do they feel that they need to make their partner agree with their reaction to the play by making the other feel guilty, stupid, or inferior. They can listen to each other and express their views freely without fearing or shaming the other. They could even go on to argue strongly about the play and could change their minds about it based on what the other person has said, not because they must change their minds to keep the peace but because they choose to. Both members of this couple would be able to have confidence in their own thoughts and feelings and be at peace with the other person having very different thoughts and feelings. They would able to be themselves and be closely connected to each other.

DIFFERENTIATION:
OUR PSYCHOLOGICAL IMMUNE SYSTEM

Our "self", our ability to manage our thoughts, feelings, and actions, makes it possible for us to stay psychologically balanced even when we are exposed to stressful life events and difficult people. Just as our physical immune system allows us to stay healthy when we are exposed to microbes that can make us sick, our "self" allows us to go through difficult and even traumatic life events and keep functioning. The more highly differentiated our self is, the more we are able to experience painful life situations and yet remain loving and productive.

The problems which have brought you to therapy have challenged your psychological immune system. Microbes which challenge your physical immune system can make you sick or they can push your immunities to become stronger. Your psychological struggles can make you sick but they can also push you to develop a stronger, more mature self. If you use therapy to become more differentiated, your symptoms will be alleviated or weakened and you will become less susceptible to future emotional difficulties.

By becoming more differentiated, you will increase your ability to form and maintain close relationships with others without becoming psychologically overwhelmed. But not with everyone! Your physical immune system is not always strong enough to handle exposure to certain germs. There are times when you need to isolate yourself from those germs in order to stay alive and to maintain your health. Similarly, you may need to isolate yourself from certain people or situations either permanently or temporarily so that you can build up your immune systems and regain your health.

THE PROCESSES OF DIFFERENTIATION

The process of differentiating a self is made up of two intertwined processes:

1. defining your self and

2.making and maintaining non-anxious connections with others.

I will explore these two processes as if they are distinct from each other, but the distinction between them is arbitrary; it is impossible to define your self without defining it to someone and it is impossible to connect non-anxiously with someone else without more clearly defining your self.

Let's look more closely at the two processes involved in differentiation. Defining your self is a lifelong, never-completed process of determining who you are, what you believe, what you value, and what your purposes in life are. It is a lifelong, never-completed process of making decisions and taking action to put those beliefs, values, and purposes into practice. It involves resisting the strong pressures around you and within you to give up your beliefs, your values, and your purposes in order to "fit in" and be like the others around you. It involves realizing that the others around you are not you and they do not need to have the same beliefs, values, and purposes that you do. It means realizing that the others around you have their own free will and cannot be controlled by you, that they are free to define themselves or not define themselves as they choose. It involves choosing to be responsible to others but realizing that you are not responsible for them.

One of the difficulties that therapy clients have in more clearly defining themselves is that they usually come to therapy hoping to change someone else or hoping that someone else will change. As we saw earlier, most people come to therapy hoping to define someone else's self, an impossible task. Therapy becomes successful only when clients turn from their original goal of changing or defining someone else to the more attainable goal of figuring out who they themselves are. It is often painful and humbling to make the transition from working on others to working on yourself but it is usually a great relief and carries with it a sense of freedom and power. It can be humbling to realize that you need to make changes in your self; at the same time, it is empowering to realize that you actually can make those changes. In moving from trying to change others to trying to change yourself, you are making a transition from an impossible task to one which is possible. No wonder it can be such a relief and carry with it such a sense of empowerment!

The other aspect of the process of differentiation is making and maintaining non-anxious connections with others, most importantly your family, past and present. This process moves you towards connecting with others in your life more clearly and honestly and with less fear, less blame, and less need to change others. It also moves you towards communicating directly with the important others in your life, without involving a third party.

THE DANCE OF DIFFERENTIATION: TWO STEPS FORWARD, ONE STEP BACK

The process of differentiating your self is not a smooth one. Even if you work as hard as you can at it, you will not steadily get better each day or each week or each year; you will experience setbacks and relapses. True change in level of differentiation or the level of any symptom is almost always a two-steps-forward-and-one-step-back process. Figure 4 presents this in graphic form.

FIGURE 4

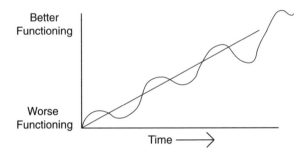

This figure indicates that people often hope that change will be a process in which they will continually get better and never have any relapses or setbacks, as illustrated by the straight line in Figure 4. This unrealistic expectation can stunt a person's growth because it eventually will lead them to give up hope in their own ability to change. Here is how this works: if Bill is trying to rid himself of his anxiety problem and he expects that his anxiety will gradually be reduced and each day or each week will be better than the one before, then he will become very discouraged when he has a day or week in which he is more anxious than he was before. He might come to believe that all his efforts to rid himself of anxiety are not working and that he should simply give up. However, if he understands that the process of change is like the wavy line in Figure 4, he will understand that his setbacks are a natural part of the process of change.

When he is doing very well (when he is at the top of one of the bumps on the wavy line) he is doing something new for him: living with less anxiety than he has for some time. This burst of change is very exciting for him and yet it is most likely temporary. He soon will face an anxiety-provoking event in his life and will become more anxious than he has been in some time. If the process of real change is happening, however, he will be able to recover more quickly than he has in the past and he will not get as anxious as he did when he experienced similar events in the past. Thus his low point (the bottom of one of the bumps on the graph) is lower than his just-experienced high but higher than his most recent low!

This two-steps-forward-one-step-back process of change is not just a frustrating inconvenience for the person trying to change. This process of change actually strengthens the changes which are being made in a way which would not happen if the process were smooth and without relapse. Let's see how this works with Bill as he struggles to become less anxious: The return of his anxiety symptoms motivates and challenges him to use the skills which he has learned to control his anxiety. If he meets the challenge, he will be able to master his fears more quickly and with a lower level of anxiety than he has in the past. His mastery of a particularly anxiety-provoking situation will make him less vulnerable to anxiety symptoms in the future. He will then experience a further reduction of symptoms until he runs into another difficult situation which increases his anxiety. Once again, he can use his skills of mastering his anxiety to pull himself out of anxiety's grip and his success will make him even less vulnerable to anxiety in the future. Each setback helps him gain more and more control over his anxiety by motivating him to get better and better at managing his anxiety. The two-steps-forward-and-one-step-back process of change can apply to all types of problems: from weight reduction to increasing motivation, from anger control to depression. It also applies to the process of the differentiation of the self.

People do not become more differentiated without setbacks. The setbacks are an important part of the process: they motivate the person to keep working (because they cause pain) and they increase the person's ability to differentiate because the person is challenged to use their new skills and insights.

DIFFERENTIATION AND YOUR FAMILY

A discussion of the differentiation of self is incomplete without exploring what happens to a family (or any other human system) when one of its members increases their level of differentiation. As we have just seen, differentiation of one's self is not done in isolation from but in connection to one's family. The more fear there is in a family, the more the members of the family (including the person working on becoming more differentiated!) will consciously or unconsciously resist the changes brought about by the one trying to differentiate.

In a relatively anxious family, when one member moves towards a higher level of differentiation, both the family and that individual will react in ways which will increase the pressure on that person to go back to the way they were and the place which they held in the family. In this way, the family tries to maintain its patterns of attachment and the position of the differentiating member in that system. In other words, when one person in a system becomes more of a self, more of an individual, the forces of togetherness in the system get stronger. The person trying to differentiate feels pressure from the others and from inside themselves to return to the way they were, conforming to the "rules" of the system.

In more personal terms, the more anxious your family is, the more your family members and you yourself will resist the changes which you are trying to make. The more anxious your family is, the more pressure you will feel from your own fears to go back to the way you were. You will be tempted to stop the process of differentiating your self. You will probably go back for a time to your old ways. But this is the dance of differentiation: two-steps-forward-and-one-step-back.

Although family members often resist the differentiation of one of its members, they can also become "infected" by it. Differentiation can be "contagious". When one family member becomes clearer about who they are and begins connecting to their family members in less fearful ways, often the others realize that if they are to have a relationship with the person who is changing, they themselves are going to have to change. In other words, when one person changes the way they are connecting to a second person, that second person must eventually change they way they connect to the first person if they are to maintain the relationship. In this way, differentiation can spread in a family.

HOW NORA MADE LASTING CHANGES

Nora entered therapy with Dr. Susan Kleinfelter because she was having anxiety attacks which she came to realize were related to her frustrations with her husband Charlie and her son Quinn. She had little confidence in herself that she could take any steps towards changing things in her family because she felt controlled by her anxiety. She was having difficulty talking to her husband and her son about important issues because, whenever she did, she would become overwhelmed with anxiety. She came to therapy hoping to get rid of her anxiety by changing those other people who were making her life miserable and found herself gently confronted by her therapist with her own need to change. After gaining some control over her anxiety by using some techniques which Dr. Kleinfelter taught her, she eventually began to work on increasing her level of differentiation (a process which she called "growing up").

In her struggle towards differentiating her self she was aided by Dr. Kleinfelter who was a relatively non-anxious, well-differentiated therapist and therefore was quite helpful to Nora. Having a relatively mature therapist made things easier; Nora and her family did not have to fight against their therapist to make positive changes!

When Nora first came to Dr. Kleinfelter, she blamed Charlie for her anxiety and for the difficulties in their family. She understood that the anxiety symptoms she was experiencing were at least in part due to her dissatisfaction with and fear about her relationships with Charlie and Quinn. Thus she was aware that there needed to be changes in her relationships with her husband and her son if she was going to get over her anxiety symptoms. Nora had an understanding that things had to change between Charlie, Quinn, and herself; her solution was to focus intensely on changing Charlie and Quinn. Early in therapy she tried to draw Dr. Kleinfelter into an alliance to force change on Charlie and Quinn but, fortunately for Nora, Dr. K politely (non-anxiously) declined her invitation to join forces with her against her husband and her son.

Dr. K helped Nora explore the patterns which existed in her current family and in her family of origin and helped Nora to draw parallels between these two parts of her extended family. Nora's focus in her therapy sessions and in the rest of her waking hours was still on trying to get Charlie to "really talk to her" and to get Quinn to take more responsibility for himself. She tried very hard to get Charlie and Quinn to heal the rift between them but got no significant results. Gradually, over a period of months, Nora began to understand that neither Charlie nor Quinn wanted to change. She began to realize that she was trying to do something which was impossible: make her husband and son act, think, and feel differently. She also came to see that by working so hard to get others to change, she was putting a great emotional burden on herself and that she was "helping" Charlie and Quinn to avoid taking responsibility for their own lives and for their relationship with each other.

One particular therapy session stood out for Nora. She began the session complaining bitterly about Charlie's lack of sensitivity towards Quinn's feelings and his verbal abuse of his son. For the three days leading up to the session she had been anxiously involved in another of Quinn's asthma attacks which she believed was brought on by Charlie's anger towards Quinn. After Charlie had yelled at his son over the phone for being a "baby" and an "irresponsible brat", Quinn began to get back at his father indirectly by beginning to smoke again and by failing to take his medication. Nora had taken several days off from work and she spent that time pleading with Quinn to take better care of himself so that his father would not be so angry with him. Her pleas were met by stony resistance by her son. She also spent many anxious hours pleading with Charlie to be more sensitive to their son. She wanted to cancel her session with Dr. K that week because she was too overwhelmed. She went to her session anyway, exhausted and furious with her husband and son. After she described to Dr. K what had been going on, the therapist paused in thought for a full minute and then asked Nora gently but pointedly, "how does your peace keeping mission seem to be working?"

Nora was devastated by realizing that she was not getting her husband and son to settle their differences. The timing was right for Nora to see that she was working very hard at something which was impossible. As her tears flowed heavily, she saw clearly that she had done the same thing in her parent's marriage: she had tried to bring together two people who were running away from each other emotionally. She also saw how she was following in her mother's footsteps by not letting her son grow up and take responsibility for his own life. In her exhaustion, frustration, and humiliation she could see that there was only one person that she could change: herself. From this point forward true change became possible because she began to see more clearly that only by working on herself would things be better for her as well as for her husband and son. She began to focus more and more on differentiating her self. Although this session was her 10th with Dr. K, she could now begin the work of making lasting changes. Therapy had truly begun. Therapy from this point on was not easy for Nora and it did not proceed in a straight line towards her becoming more differentiated. However, for Nora, lasting change became possible because she was ready to work on herself.

As therapy proceeded, she began to be more acutely aware of how much she blamed Charlie and Quinn for her unhappiness. She began to see more and more clearly how much she told herself that if only they were different, she would be able to have a good life. In visits to her mother she heard for the first time what she had listened to for many years: her mother complaining that if only her husband had not divorced her and if only her 44-year-old son Steven would have straightened himself out, she would have had a much better life. Nora began to see how she was following closely behind her mother in a multi-generational parade of women who depended for their happiness on husbands who emotionally ran away and sons who never left home.

These insights about herself were both painful and freeing for Nora. They were painful because she realized how much of her time she had wasted in the fruitless pursuit of her husband. They were painful because she realized how her over-protection of Quinn had made it more difficult for him to grow up and become a man. And they were painful because she was not sure if she could make the changes in herself which she needed to because the patterns were so ingrained in her.

These insights were freeing to her because she realized that she did not have to wait for Charlie to change so that she would feel better. They were freeing because she realized that she did not have to wait for Quinn to take responsibility for himself. She no longer needed to mire herself in the blame of others and the shame she felt that she was a failure as a wife and mother. She also realized that for many years she had been avoiding figuring out what her own life was about by focusing so totally on her husband and her son.

She began to take responsibility in a new way for her long-standing problems with anxiety. She had always told herself, "When Charlie becomes a better husband and father and when Quinn gets settled and on his own, I won't worry so much." Now she was telling herself that it was her own thoughts that were making her anxious and that she could learn to think about things differently so that she wouldn't have to be so anxious. She saw for the first time that she was the one who was making herself anxious, not anyone else. She realized that when she did make herself

anxious it was generally because she was taking responsibility for Charlie or for Quinn and that she didn't need to do
so. She started telling herself that Quinn's asthma belonged
to him and it was his to deal with, not hers. She became
aware that Charlie could decide what he wanted from their
marriage and that he could decide whether or not he wanted to make changes. She saw clearly that Quinn and
Charlie were responsible to work out their relationship and
that she needed to stay out of their way.

All these new thoughts began to reduce the frequency and severity of her anxiety problems and she began to
feel more in control of her self and her own emotions. She
knew she was not out of the woods yet because whenever
she fell back into her old ways of thinking, she would get
very anxious and her anxiety would be a signal that she
needed to work on herself and her own thinking rather than
trying to change others. Her fear became helpful to her as a
spur to change her thoughts and her actions.

With Dr. K.'s help and guidance, she began to take
firmer and less fearful stands with Charlie and with Quinn.
She matter-of-factly told Charlie that she had been striving
for many years to get him to be a better father to Quinn. She
said she was going to try very hard to "resign from the job"
of trying to force him to be a better father. She let him know
that she had finally realized that the conflicts and struggles
between Charlie and Quinn were for them to work out and
that she was going to work very hard to not get between
them. She admitted to Charlie that she would not be immediately successful in staying out of the middle and that she
would probably find herself in the middle again. But she
made it clear to him that she intended to remove herself
from the middle as soon as she found herself there. She
focused on what she was going to do rather than talking to

Charlie about what he should do. After so many years of arguing about how to handle their son, this was a new conversation. No longer was Nora berating Charlie for his faults or pleading with him to be different. She was quietly but with great resolve telling him where she was headed.

Charlie was surprised by this conversation and sensed that somehow Nora was different and more powerful than she had ever been. He was relieved that Nora was "off his case" but he was also uneasy that he might have to do something different now that she was so different. Then he comforted himself with the thought that this was just something Nora was going through because she was seeing Dr. K and that she would soon drop this new way of acting and go back to criticizing him and pleading with him. He figured that he shouldn't worry about what she had told him and that he was just fine the way he was.

Quinn's next crisis set Nora back and also provided her with a great opportunity. Quinn's smoking and skipping his medication precipitated another serious asthma attack which resulted in a late night trip to the emergency room and a stay in the hospital. Charlie refused to visit Quinn in the hospital saying to Nora that the kid needed to "grow up" and that he, Charlie, was "sick of the whole thing." Nora dropped everything and drove the two hours to the town where Quinn was in college. On the way there, she had an intense desire to comfort Quinn and a strong sense that she needed to protect him from his father's anger. She came to Quinn's room in the hospital feeling burdened with responsibility for Quinn's health and feeling sorry for him that his father was being such a jerk. She also had in the back of her mind what Dr. K. had said (too many times): "Charlie is responsible for Charlie and Quinn is responsible for Quinn". She also heard Dr. K's voice saying, "I wonder if you're ready to get out of their way." (She hated it when Dr. K said things like that!)

At Quinn's bedside she felt very confused and anxious, not knowing what to do. She talked to Quinn in her usual soothing tones but she was also aware of her anger towards her son because he kept doing foolish and self-destructive things which seemed to force her to drop everything in her life and run to his side. She began to see him as a young man who was hurting himself rather than as a helpless boy who was the victim of his father and his disease. She decided to take a walk down to the hospital coffee shop to think about what she should do. She did not want to do what she had usually done (pity Quinn and side with him against his father) although she was very tempted to do so because all of her old feelings and thoughts were back. She wanted to think things through in a new way and to express to both Quinn and Charlie in a caring but firm way that they were responsible for themselves and that she loved them but was resigning from the job of caretaker. Sitting over her cup of coffee, she came up with a plan, a way to approach this current crisis in a new way.

When she returned to Quinn's room, he looked pale and frightened and her heart sank with pity. In spite of her strong desire to take care of and protect him, she proceeded with her plan. She told Quinn that she was frightened and concerned for him but that she was also angry with him for not taking care of his asthma. She told him that she had recently become aware that she had felt responsible for his asthma and had been trying to rescue him from it ever since he was a little boy. She told him she was going to try to stop feeling responsible for him and stop feeling guilty about him. She said that she believed that he would do a better job of dealing with his asthma if she stayed out of it. She also told him that she was going to try not to worry about how he and his dad were getting along because she believed that the two of them would work out their relationship as they decided. Quinn, like his father before him, was surprised by the new tenor of his mother's remarks and felt both relieved and frightened. Nora went on to say that she loved him very much and would always love him but that what he did with his asthma was up to him.

She was about to leave the room when the phone rang and Quinn picked up the receiver: it was his father. Nora could tell from the pained look on her son's face and the sharp but muffled crackling coming from the phone that Charlie was beginning to angrily criticize his son for being so stupid as to let his asthma get out of hand and cause him to wind up in the hospital. She imagined that Charlie was telling Quinn how much this was going to cost Charlie and how he probably wouldn't finish college because he was such a screwed up kid. Nora stopped at the door and watched her son get paler and more silently, sullenly angry. Instinctively, she wanted to rip the phone out of her son's hand and yell at Charlie to leave Quinn alone. It took all her strength to walk over to Quinn's bed, kiss him on the forehead and say "I love you" before turning and walking out the door and out of the hospital. Her tears were tears of pain and sadness but also of relief.

When she arrived home, there was a message on her answering machine. It was Quinn's voice, obviously pained and weak, asking why she had left so soon and why she was being so selfish as to turn and walk out on him. Her pangs of guilt were strong within her and her first impulse was to call him back and apologize to him and tell him she would be back the next day. But she stopped herself and thought about what she was trying to do with both Quinn and Charlie and how she needed to do something *other than follow her knee-jerk reactions. She composed herself and thought through again how Quinn was capable of handling his asthma and his father and that her helping him was not helpful. She then called him back and asked him how his phone call with his father had gone (she knew this would be a difficult subject for her to handle calmly, but she had the courage to jump right into the deep end!). Quinn began by saying that his father was such a jerk and didn't understand how difficult things were for Quinn and how lousy he felt and how bad his asthma was.*

Nora felt the familiar pull to rush to Quinn's side to comfort him and agree with him that his father was indeed a jerk but she caught herself. She heard herself saying, "Well, that's your dad. I guess you guys will find some way of getting along without killing each other."

She then changed the subject to how he was doing physically and he began to complain about how the nurses were not helping him enough and how tired he felt and how discouraged he was that he kept ending up in the hospital. He asked her if she was coming to visit him tomorrow. She heard the fear and the pleading in his voice. She told him that she would visit him the following weekend after he got out of the hospital because there were things she had to take care of at home.

"And besides," she said, "I trust you'll figure out how to get the doctors and nurses to help you." He started to talk again about his dad and what a jerk he was because he just yelled at him instead of helping him and she said, "I don't know what you guys are going to do" and changed the subject. They talked for a few more minutes about things that Quinn wanted her to bring when she came to visit him, Nora said she needed to go, said "I love you", and Quinn snarled, "Yeah, sure".

Nora again felt the pangs of guilt and fear and her anxiety symptoms began acting up. Her palms got sweaty, her breathing became more rapid and shallower, and she felt a little light-headed. She did some breathing and relaxation exercises which Dr. K. had taught her and she felt better as her symptoms gradually disappeared but the guilt and the concern for her son remained. She told herself that he needed to take care of his asthma himself and that, as Dr., K predicted, she would have a difficult time letting go. She told herself that she was on the right track and that the anxiety she was feeling was a normal part of her getting better and the result of her taking a new tack with her husband and her son. She decided that she needed to go somewhere to gather herself and to reflect on the painful and challenging events of the past few days. She made up her mind to go to one of her favorite places, the city's cathedral, to think and maybe even to pray (she was not a particularly religious woman). She always felt encouraged and thoughtful when she spent time in the cathedral. As she sat there in the cool, dark sanctuary thinking about the changes she was struggling to make, her fears subsided even more and she was able to see that she had done some good work that day.

The next day, Charlie called and wanted to find out if the two of them were going to get together that evening. Nora and Charlie had been separated for about six months and their relationship was very uneasy. Neither of them were clear about what the "rules" were regarding how often they would see each other, whether he could come over to the house without calling, whether they would spend all weekend nights together, and whether or not they would have sex. Nora was irritated that Charlie had called but she did want to see him. She wanted to see him partly to blast

him for the way he talked to Quinn on the phone and partly to see how he was coping emotionally with their separation. They agreed to meet for dinner at a favorite restaurant
of theirs at 7:00. As Nora prepared herself mentally for this
meeting (or was it a date?), she vacillated between rework-
ing her familiar speech which showed him what an insensitive jerk he was with his son and thinking through how she
could be different than she ever had with him. She liked
how she felt after her talk with him a few days earlier when
she told him what she was working on and how she was
going to try to stay out of taking responsibility for him and
for his relationship with Quinn. She decided she wanted to
follow up on that talk and try to put herself again in that
position.

Charlie was charming at dinner and rather flirta-
tious with her which both pleased her and caused her to
wonder how she was being set up. She told herself, "He
really is a great guy and I can just be myself with him."
However, as the conversation turned to Quinn, he began
showing his anger and disgust with their son and with her
running to the hospital to "hold his hand". She felt her
speech about his insensitivity to Quinn forming in her mind
and approaching her tongue when she decided just to listen
to what he had to say and not to try to influence how he
was thinking. This was quite a struggle for her as lines from
her state of the husband address kept running through her
mind.

Finally, she said, "You know, Charlie, I've been trying for years to get you to see Quinn differently and to talk
to him more respectfully but I've decided to give up on that
project. You two will see each other the way you see each
other. It is very hard for me to listen to your criticism of
Quinn and I would appreciate it if we could move on to other

things." Charlie asked her if she had learned these lines "from your shrink" which caused Nora a momentary pang of doubt but she moved ahead with the conversation and they managed to have a pleasant dinner. They went home separately to their own houses.

Nora was scheduled to see Dr. K. several days after her dinner with Charlie. As the appointment approached, Nora felt excited by all the new things she had tried and was hoping that Dr. K. would also be excited by her progress. She told Dr. K about her work with Charlie and with Quinn and how she felt so much better because she was realizing for the first time in her life in such a profound way that she had choices. She felt lighter and freer. She felt less burdened by the guilt, worry, and anxiety which she had carried with her for all of her adult life. She told Dr. K that she was struggling to maintain her new ways of acting and thinking and that she had won some important victories.

Dr. K was obviously pleased and excited for Nora and supported her ongoing struggle for change. Dr. K also warned her that Charlie and Quinn would probably do something which would tempt Nora to go back to her old ways, not because they were cruelly manipulating her to go back to the way she was, but simply because that's the way people work. She reminded Nora that any change by one person in a family moving towards differentiation is met by a counter-force pulling all the members of the family back towards the status quo. She joked that this was "Kleinfelter's First Law of Psychodynamics".

A few minutes later, Dr. K steered the conversation towards Nora's relationship with her parents and looked for parallels between those relationships and what was happening among the threesome of herself, Charlie, and Quinn.

She suggested that Nora have a talk with each of her parents about her struggles and ask them if they had struggled with problems similar to hers. Nora left the session feeling better than she had in years but puzzled and apprehensive about Dr. K.'s suggestion of talking with her parents.

She put off calling her mother for a week or so because she was afraid to talk with her about Quinn and Charlie. She knew that her mother would begin blaming her ex-husband (Nora's father) and move to fretting about her son Steven and Nora's son Quinn. She cursed Dr. K under her breath as she thought about talking to her mother even though she knew that she had to. She knew that she needed to work on becoming less afraid of and emotionally dependent upon her parents. Finally, she managed to gather enough courage together to call her mother. They spoke first of the pleasantries and superficial news of their lives and, as this went on for several minutes, Nora began to get more and more nervous. She felt her palms become sweaty, her heart race, and her breathing become quicker and shallower. She took a deep breath and told her mother she was learning some things from Dr. Kleinfelter about her relationships with Charlie and Quinn. Her mother said she didn't understand why she needed to make any changes with her husband and her son because they were the real problem. "After all," she said, "poor Quinn has asthma and can't help that and, besides, Charlie is like most men: they're not much help with family problems. He's just like your father."

Nora wanted this conversation with her mother to go in a different direction than had so many of their conversations down through the years. She said, "I know, Mom. Charlie is somewhat like dad--he's got a temper and won't really talk with me. But I've decided to try to not criticize him or preach to him so much about how he should be with me and with Quinn."

Her mother instantly felt criticized because she recognized that both she and her daughter dealt with their men in quite similar ways. "Sounds like you're going to be letting him get away with a lot," Nora's mother said. "Charlie will figure that he can do anything he wants."

Nora felt both her anger and her anxiety mounting within her and her resolve to stay cool with her mother disappeared. "But Charlie really can do anything he wants, he's a grown man! I've got to let him go instead of trying to force him to change. Don't you see that?" By now Nora was pleading with her mother and feeling very frustrated because her mother was not agreeing with her. "Damn it, Mom," she blurted out, "you want me to blame and criticize Charlie just like you did to dad. And look where that got you!" She had never spoken so forcefully to her mother before. She was seething.

Her mother felt the attack and backed away. "You have no right to talk to me that way, Nora! You don't understand what happened between your father and me and if you did you wouldn't talk to me that way. As far as I'm concerned, this conversation is over." She hung up.

Nora felt horrible for the way the conversation had gone. She knew it had started well and that she had good intentions for it to be a time of mutual sharing rather than a blaming session, but it had so rapidly escalated into a battle of sharp tongues that even she had been taken by surprise. She was determined to mend her relationship with her mother but she knew that she had taken a step backwards in that process. She remembered Dr. K's words that change is a two-step-forward-one-step-back process. So this is what a step back feels like! Damn!

At her next session with Dr. K, Nora wanted to talk

about her feelings and thoughts surrounding her encounter with her mother because she wanted to get things right between herself and her mother. Dr. K praised her for her "gutsy" efforts to talk with her mother and for her tenacious dedication to change. They talked about Nora's stored-up anger towards her mother for being so critical of her father and for driving him away. Nora had always seen her father as the victim and her mother as the villain in their divorce. Nora began to see that she was involved in an intense triangle involving her mother and her father. This triangle was fueled at least in part by her blaming her mother and her emotionally protecting her father. She also began to see the intense triangle between herself, her son, and her husband. This triangle was fueled at least in part by her blaming her husband and her emotionally protecting her son. She stopped in her tracks: "Oh my God," she blurted out, "I'm doing the same thing all over again!" Nora was humbled by this insight but also empowered by it; she was now clearer about what she needed to work on and felt more confident in her ability to do so.

Dr. K pointed out to her that she could work on her self in the Nora-Charlie-Quinn triangle or she could work on her self in the Nora-mom-dad triangle because the triangles were remarkably similar. Dr. K smiled when she pointed out to Nora how she was surrounded with great opportunities to work on her own growth! Wherever she turned, she could work on her own differentiation. Nora laughed, too, and wondered how she had gotten so lucky!

Nora's work on herself went on for several more years. She saw Dr. K. less and less frequently as time went on. For a while she saw her once a month, then once every two months and then just when she needed a boost to help her over a difficult spot in the road. She continued to talk with her mother and father about their extended family. She found out from her mother that her father had been having an affair for several years leading up to the time of their divorce and that her mother had never told anyone in the family about it before. Nora became very angry with her father and her first impulse was to have nothing more to do with him. However, after a few months and several trips to the cathedral, she knew she needed to talk with him.

She spent an entire weekend with him talking about his marriage to her mother, the family he grew up in, and the family they were in now. This weekend was emotionally exhausting but also very helpful to her and to her father. She began to lighten up with her mother and learned not to blame her for all the problems in their family. She learned about her mother's abusive upbringing which helped her gain more understanding of and compassion for her mother. She felt gradually stronger and stronger in her interactions with her parents. She felt less and less like a child with them as time went on.

Eventually, she and Charlie together began to work on their marriage. Charlie began to see that Nora was not going to keep blaming him but that she was unlikely to stay with him unless he made some significant changes. He was angry about this and expressed that anger by having a brief affair with a woman significantly younger than himself. (He never told Nora about this affair.) He realized, however, that he was still in love with Nora. He realized he needed to talk to her without running away and that he needed to work on his anger towards her if he were to preserve the relationship. He agreed to see Dr. Kleinfelter with Nora to work on their marriage.

Both were at first quite nervous about meeting with her together: Charlie felt that he would be blamed by Dr. K for being such an insensitive jerk. He figured that Nora had been filling her head with all his faults and that she would see him as a really sick man. Nora was afraid that she would begin to blame Charlie and criticize him unmercifully in the session. This would clearly risk the wrath of Dr. K. She was very invested in being a good therapy client for Dr. K.! Their work together with Dr. K was very successful as they both learned to relax more with each other and be clearer in their communications with each other. Slowly, humor and affection began creeping back into their relationship. They both lowered their expectations that the other was going to be exactly what they wanted and began to forge a solid, accepting, and understanding bond with each other.

Nora did a lot of work on her relationship with Quinn as well. As expected, after he was hospitalized and Nora left him (so selfishly!) while he was being yelled at on the phone by his dad, Quinn continued to have crises with his asthma. It got so bad that Quinn, who was usually a very conscientious student, began failing some classes because he was sick so much. Nora struggled greatly with her instinct to protect and rescue him and then told him that he could fail if he chose to and that he probably would if he continued to smoke and not take his medication as prescribed.

Quinn dropped out of college for a semester and lived with his mother for several months. Nora felt a great deal of pressure to take care of Quinn and overprotect him during that time but she did insist that he get a job and pay her rent while he was living there. Quinn became clearer about the value of an education after working the night shift in a convenience store and returned to college where he was able to handle his health and his studies fairly well. He found that the type of women he was attracted to changed from those who took pity on him and wanted to mother him to those who respected him as a healthy, smart, and capable young man. Who can tell what the next generation will bring!

Nora also became clearer about what she wanted to do with her work life. After years of working as a secretary at a local grade school, she was able to retire and pursue her first love, gardening, full time. She got involved in a local horticultural society and volunteered at an arboretum. She had always wanted to pursue this interest but was too afraid that Charlie and Quinn could not survive without her. She not only had the time but also the mental freedom to pursue what was of great value to her. Her panic attacks and anxiety spells would occasionally begin to rise to the surface.

She found that she could dispel her anxiety by taking time to think through what was happening in her life and finding ways to be clearer about who she was and to make non-anxious connections with her important others. Her occasional visits to the cathedral encouraged and challenged her to keep going down the road she knew was hers.

Her sessions with Dr. Kleinfelter had so far extended over 2 years. Nora had seen Dr. K by herself 30 times and with Charlie eight times. For now, both Nora and Charlie felt that they had benefited greatly from therapy and they believed they were done in their work with Dr. K. As we shall see, they did return.

Six Pearls of Wisdom About Differentiation:

1. To increase your level of differentiation, you must move away from blaming others and trying to change them and move towards mastering your

own thoughts, feelings, and actions. You need to move towards taking responsibility for you rather than taking responsibility for others. You need to work on the difficult task of figuring out what is really important for you in your life.

2. Increasing your level of differentiation requires you to make and maintain less anxious connections with your family members. This means making clear your stands on important issues (without trying to make others agree with you) and becoming less afraid of your family members. It means extracting yourself from between two parties who are in conflict with each other and, at the same time, maintaining honest, relaxed, and even humorous contact with both parties.

3. If you increase your level of differentiation, you and your family members will consciously or unconsciously act in ways which will pressure you to go back to the way you were before.

4. When you meet the resistance of yourself and your family members, you will retreat, then feel more pain, and then you might be motivated to continue working towards differentiation. The dance of differentiation is two steps forward and one step back!

5. When you persist towards differentiating yourself in the face of the resistance from yourself and your family, sometimes other family members will move towards differentiation.Differentiation can becontagious!

6. If you work towards differentiation, there will be both costs and rewards. The costs will be fear, uncertainty, and pain. Eventually, the rewards will be a lightening of your burden of guilt, an increase in your level of inner peace, a greater sense of freedom to make choices, and an increased ability to handle future life difficulties.

Chapter 6

Differentiation (Part II):
How to Maintain the Changes You've Made

As we have just seen in Nora's story, when clients have made significant changes in therapy, the most natural tendency in the world is for them to be drawn back to the patterns of thinking, feeling, and relating to others which brought them to therapy in the first place. This does not mean that they will return to those patterns permanently, but it is natural for them to feel forces from inside themselves and from those close to them to go back to their old, more familiar ways. The power of the past is great and acts like a magnetic force drawing people back to their old ways.

Because your tendencies to return to your old ways may be very strong, it is essential to understand how you can maintain the (sometimes fragile) progress you have made. The best way for you to maintain your hard-won changes is to continue *to work on your own differentiation even when the problems and the pain which brought you to therapy are gone.*

Most apparently successful therapy clients end treatment when their symptoms disappear or at least become less powerful. Both therapist and client experience the treatment as successful and feel good about the outcome. However, the powerful and natural forces of the past both inside and outside the client often cause them to relapse, bringing them back to the symptoms and to the psychological pain which they had when they first sought treatment. Often, when their symptoms and pain return, these clients go back to therapy once again. They may repeat this process numerous times without understanding how their symptoms and pain fit into their life and without making the changes in themselves and their relationships which would prevent a return to their previous difficulties.

If you continue to work on your level of differentiation after your symptoms are gone and after you are no longer in acute psychological pain, then you are less likely to go through this painful and repetitive process of relapsing. There is a reason many clients stop working on their level of differentiation when their pain is gone: without their pain they are no longer motivated to make changes. Remember, people need to be in pain in order to seek change in the first place! Working on differentiating your self becomes very difficult because you have no pain to keep prodding you towards new and better ways.

One way to maintain the changes you make is to keep yourself in enough pain so that you will be motivated to work on yourself! As long as you are moderately miserable, you will be more interested in continuing the process of change. There is another way which is more difficult but less painful: work on differentiating yourself even though you are feeling relatively good. You can only do this if you understand how the problems which led you to therapy in the first place are connected to the ways you think and to your relationships with others, particularly your family members.

Often clients go through therapy and rid themselves of their symptoms (through various psychotherapeutic techniques or psychiatric medication) without understanding how those symptoms play a part in their lives and in their relationships. At the end of treatment, they are relatively symptom-free but have not understood what changes they may need to make in order to maintain those changes. They are quite susceptible to relapse because they have neither understood nor worked on the conditions which are fueling their symptoms.

By contrast, other clients realize that they must work on themselves even after their pain is mostly gone. For example, consider the client who realizes that her recurrent depression which brought her to therapy in the first place has been an integral part of her relationships with her parents, her spouse, and her children because her depression "helps" to keep her in a subservient role with them. That client would need to work not just on ridding herself of her depressive symptoms, but also on changing her subservient position in her family. She would have a better chance of preventing a relapse into depression because she would realize that unless she made some changes in her thinking and her relationships, the conditions would be right for a return to depression.

What changes do you need to make in your thinking and your relationships to prevent relapse? You need to continue to work on the two intertwined aspects of differentiation which we discussed in Chapter 5: (1) defining self more clearly and (2) connecting non-anxiously with important others. You can benefit from working with a well-differentiated therapist on a periodic but infrequent basis (say, once every month or two) in order to help stay focused on your process of differentiation. This presumes, of course, that your therapist understands your need for continued work even when your symptoms are gone. Not all therapists understand this.

Many therapists will tell their clients who have made some significant changes that they have done so well that they do not need to work on themselves anymore.

Some therapists tell their clients has done good work on themselves but that their family members are still "sick" or "dysfunctional". They often tell the client that they will be able to maintain their changes as long as they get away from or stay away from those family members who are harmful to them.

This message is usually impossible for clients to follow because they, like all of us, are attached to our families. Not only is it impossible for clients to truly separate from their families, but the message that they should do so solidifies a bond between therapist and client against the client's "others" causing the therapy triangle to become stuck.

This stuck therapy triangle makes the client more likely to relapse. If the client sees him- or herself as "healthier" than the "others" then they are likely to either run away from their family (emotionally or geographically) or work very hard to "confront" their family members in an effort to force them to change. If the client runs away from their family, the client avoids facing their own difficult issues and misses out on many opportunities to become more differentiated. If the client tries to change their family members, those "others" are likely to be very frustrated by his or her efforts to force them to change and, as a result, they are likely to blame or pull away from the client. The client is faced with a very painful dilemma: they can then either cut off from those family members or they can return to their old ways of connecting with their family, the ways which led them to be symptomatic and seek therapy in the first place. A therapist who sides with clients against their "others" will not be helpful to clients who are trying to prevent a return to their problems and their pain.

By contrast, a therapist who understands that the

client needs to keep working on defining self and making non-anxious connections with their family in order to maintain their still fragile gains is much more helpful. At this stage of therapy, clients need a therapist who understands their need to focus on changing themselves and not on changing others. Clients need a therapist who will blame neither the client nor their family but will accept and value both. As we saw previously, the most helpful therapist is the mature therapist.

What can you do in this phase of therapy to keep growing? By continuing to focus on differentiating yourself in spite of the many distractions which life provides. It is important to remember that if you slip backwards, you will again experience pain, perhaps in the form of the symptoms which led you to therapy in the first place. At that time, you may be motivated to work more on yourself. To understand this process more clearly, let's return to Nora and her therapeutic work to provide us with an example of this "relapse prevention" phase of therapy. Remember, however, that the way Nora worked on her differentiation may be different from yours.

NORA STRUGGLES TO MAINTAIN HER CHANGES

When we last left Nora, she was doing quite well and had made some significant changes. She had nearly eliminated her anxiety symptoms and had made some very significant changes in her relationships with her husband, her son, her mother, and her father.

She understood how her anxiety was connected to her thinking about herself and others and connected to her relationships to these significant people in her life. She had also been able to make a change in her work life so that she was doing something much more satisfying to her.

It would seem that she might be immune to relapse because she had made so much progress! If only change were so easy!

In her relationship with her husband Charlie, she found herself increasingly irritated by his distancing from her. Their relationship had significantly improved and their separation had been helpful to them in learning to appreciate and tolerate each other better. Charlie was still very uncomfortable with Nora's newfound strength and happiness. He felt inferior to her because she was doing so well. The more he felt inferior, the more he pulled away from her. When Charlie pulled away from her, she became more and more afraid that he would keep distancing from her. Her first instinct was to nag him to open up to her more. She had learned, however, that criticizing and nagging him in an attempt to get him to open up was not only futile but also counter-productive. She knew that she and Charlie would pull apart until the next crisis in their life brought them together in frustration and anger. She did not want to go down that road again so she began to think about how she could connect differently with Charlie. She wanted to find a way to clearly define herself to him without telling him what to do. She decided to be as honest and non-controlling as possible.

She found a time with Charlie where they could unhurriedly talk things through without interruption and, as that time approached, she worked hard to keep her fear and anxiety in check. She began by telling Charlie how much she loved him and how important he was to her. She went on to say that she was very frightened by how he seemed to be pulling away from her. She said that she was afraid that he would leave her and that she didn't want that at all. She also said that she knew that Charlie could do whatev-

er he wanted in their relationship but that she hoped he would decide to open up to her. She said that she was working on containing her own fear and her own tendency to try to make Charlie love her. She also clearly stated that she wanted to be close to him but could not force him.

Charlie did not respond to her immediately. For several days he said nothing to her about what was going on with him. Eventually, he screwed up enough courage to sit her down and tell her that he thought he was depressed and had been for many years. He was very frustrated by the way his career had gone and now all he could do was to hang on for the last four years until he could retire. He said he just felt burned out and discouraged. He also told her for the first time that he was frightened by the changes she had made. He was glad that she was happier but her happiness only made him feel more frustrated. He told her that her happiness made him jealous and angry; he knew he could get back at her by pulling away and not talking to her.

Nora was relieved that Charlie's problems were no more serious. She felt very glad that he had opened up to her about things which had been troubling him for years. She also felt the urge to "help" Charlie by recommending a whole list of things that he could do to get better. All she said was "I'm glad you told me. I've got faith in you that you will do what you need to do to figure this out." He asked her what she thought he should do and she said that she didn't know. She added, "I only know what was helpful to me." Finally she told him she loved him and said she would be glad to talk with him at any time about how he was doing.

Charlie was a bit shocked that she did not tell him what to do or begin lecturing to him even though she had not been like that with him for several years. He still expected *her to anxiously plead with him to change. He would know what to do then: he would anxiously and angrily pull away from her. But now he didn't know quite what to do. He would have to think about it.*

Nora felt good about how she was handling things with Charlie but she decided to go back to Dr. Kleinfelter for a few sessions to sort through her thoughts and feelings. She had not been to see Dr. K for about two years. Dr. K. listened carefully and supported her in how well she had handled things with Charlie. At the end of the session, she suggested that Nora spend some time with her father because her father and Nora had a connection which was similar to her connection with Charlie. Nora felt a pang of fear run through her. She knew Dr. K. had hit on something important but she was not clear what it was.

A month later, she was able to get some time with her father: it took a while even though they lived only an hour apart and her father was retired. She had felt distant from her dad lately as he had not been calling her or visiting her as much as he had previously. Her father was now 79 years old, in declining health, and lonely. He had remarried after his divorce from Nora's mother but that marriage lasted less than five years. He was bitter that he had ended up alone at this stage in his life; he was a rather frustrated and lonely old man. Her first instincts when she realized he was in this condition were to try to get him to look on the bright side of things and to get the medical attention that he needed. She wanted to cheer him up and show him that he could be happy if only he would open up to her and to his friends. She had all kinds of suggestions for him. She also felt her anger rising towards him because he had spent his life running away from closeness with others and now he was complaining about being alone. She was afraid that he would soon die a lonely old man.

Nora had not been with her dad long when she realized that her reaction to him was very much like her reaction to Charlie. Both men pulled away from others when they needed help, both were silently depressed a good deal of the time and both needed her help! She realized that what she needed to do was to connect with her father in a very different way than she had before. She had always felt that she was responsible for helping him to be different and making him love her.

She had always wanted to impress him with her achievements and take care of him so well that he would express his appreciation to her. Usually, however, he would lapse into his sullen depression.

Nora realized with Dr. K.'s help that she needed to connect with her father more often and in a non-anxious way, a way which was not filled with her own desire to change this old man. She began visiting him regularly, caring for him in his sicknesses, but not taking responsibility for him. She told him often that she loved him and she gradually gave up on her hopes that he would be a happy, vibrant man. She heard him talk with some bitterness about his upbringing in a rather cold and unemotional family where he never felt special. For the first time she saw a lonely little boy when she looked at her father; a lonely little boy who was the "father" to this old man. She understood that the way he was now was the way he was going to be and that she did not need to pressure him to be any different. Emotionally, she began to let him go but continued to show her love for him. A few months later he died with Nora at his bedside and with his other children having said their goodbyes. Nora grieved deeply but knew that she had done what she could.

While she was spending time with her father during his last days, her feelings for Charlie changed. She saw in

Charlie the angry and hurt boy that he had been and she began in a new way to let him go and love him also. She no longer demanded even within herself that he be different. She knew deeply that he was who he was. Oddly enough, Charlie began to soften towards Nora and to open up to her more. He actually began to show his love for her as he had never done before. She had a sense of how difficult this was for him and so she appreciated it more. A growing sense of peace was slowly invading Nora's life.

Nora had successfully fought off a relapse into anxiety, fear, and anger by dealing with Charlie's depression and distance in a new way. A big part of this was dealing with her father's depression and distance in a new way. She worked on her own tendency to react in anger, fear, and exaggerated "helpfulness" and had found a new way to connect with these two very important men in her life. She had avoided relapse and had grown from it. The pain of her relationship with Charlie had helped move her to a new place with Charlie, with her father, and with herself. She was not finished growing. Life was not done with her. She would have more pains and difficult connections with others. But through her work on herself, learning to be herself and connect with others calmly, she was stronger than ever in her ability to handle herself. Peace had come to Nora as it never had before.

Pearl of Wisdom: Don't stop therapy when you have just begun to get better. If you continue to work on your level of differentiation after your symptoms and pain are much better, you are less likely to relapse and you are much more likely to achieve lasting changes in your life.

Chapter 7

Potential Aides to Lasting Change:
Techniques and Medication

Although therapy clients need to increase their level of differentiation to make significant and lasting changes in their life, when they come to therapy they are often in too much pain to do the difficult work of differentiation. As we saw in Chapter 2, people need to be in some psychological pain to be motivated enough to do the difficult work necessary to make such lasting changes. However, many clients initially are in too much pain to do the work that may lie ahead of them.

Psychological pain has a complicated relationship to therapy: if the client has too little pain, they will not be motivated to make any changes; if the client has too much pain they will not be able to make any changes. The symptoms of clients who are in too much pain disable and preoccupy them so that they are not able to work effectively on differentiating. In these cases, what clients need are ways to reduce the intensity of their pain so that they can move forward. They need techniques to enable them to be free enough of their symptoms to do the difficult work that is required to make lasting changes. Fortunately, professionals have developed many therapeutic techniques and many types of medication which can help clients reduce their level of distress.

When Nora first came to see Dr. Kleinfelter, she was so overwhelmed by her anxiety attacks that she was unable to make the changes in her life which would eventually free her from anxiety. Dr. K used some relaxation training and other anxiety management techniques to help

Nora control her anxiety and to lessen their power over her life. These techniques (which we will discuss more fully in a later section of this chapter) helped her gain control over her fears and made it possible for her to work on the difficult task of resolving the problems in her life with herself, her son, her husband, and her parents. For Nora, these anxiety management techniques were not the whole of therapy or even the major focus. They were, however, a very important part of her treatment because they made it possible for her to work on the task of differentiating herself in the midst of her family.

There are far too many therapeutic techniques and psychiatric medications to list in this chapter, let alone to discuss in depth. By the time the list was completed it would be obsolete; there would be newly devised techniques and medications ready to be added.

In this chapter, I have chosen to simplify the discussion of symptom-reduction strategies by discussing just four of the most proven types of interventions. I hope to make clear how such techniques can reduce the power of client's symptoms, improve their sense of self-mastery, and, as a result, enable them to work on their own differentiation. Although some of these techniques and some medications can have dramatically positive results, it is important to keep in mind that none of them are "magic cures." They do not work for everyone, all of them require that the person making the changes have some motivation to change, and all of them bump up against the power of the past. In addition, even the most effective of these symptom-reduction strategies can actually slow down or prevent any lasting change in the individual or in the family because of problems in the therapy triangle. I have chosen four types of symptom reduction interventions to focus on in this chapter because they are well researched, proven effective for many and they are very widely practiced in the mental health field:

1. Cognitive techniques
2. Anxiety management techniques
3. Behavioral management strategies for child behavior problems
4. Psychiatric medication

Most popular discussions of therapy focus more on techniques than I am doing in this book. Most of the material written for the general public about psychotherapy says that this technique will work with this problem and that technique will work with that problem. The public is even subjected to the grandiose claims of some therapists who say that their techniques will work for all clients no matter what their problems are. It is clear to me that there are many helpful techniques to reduce symptoms but their effectiveness is based not only on the merits of that technique but also on the handling of the therapy triangle by the therapist, the client, and the "other".

COGNITIVE THERAPY TECHNIQUES

Cognitive therapy is a set of techniques based on the simple, straightforward notion that the way you think about yourself and the world profoundly influences your feelings. Since such disorders as depression and anxiety involve very painful feelings, this approach is designed to help the client identify and change those ways of thinking which are causing the feelings involved in depression and anxiety. This type of therapy is based also on the notion that events do not directly cause feelings; a person's feelings are caused by the way they think about those events. Figure 5 presents this in graphic form:

FIGURE 5

Events automatically trigger thoughts about those events and these automatic thoughts in turn cause the person to have feelings about those events. For example, a boss criticizes his employee for his recent performance and that employee "gets depressed". The boss criticizing the employee is the event and the employee's "depression" is the feeling. The criticizing, however did not cause the employee to feel depressed, it was the way the employee thought about the criticism. In this case, the employee thought, "I really can't do anything right. I really screwed this up because I'm so stupid. Damn it, when am I ever going to learn?" As the employee thought these kinds of thoughts over and over he became more and more depressed. In reaction to the same criticism, another employee might say to himself, "I realize I made a mistake and the boss was right to point that out to me. I haven't made a big mistake like this in a while. I guess I need to pay more attention next time. Over all, I still think I'm doing a good job." The second employee would end up feeling better about himself than the first while not neglecting the fact that he made a mistake. The first employee would end up feeling depressed, the second would not.

Cognitive therapy has been extensively and carefully researched and has been shown to be helpful for many people particularly those suffering from depression, anxiety, and problems managing their anger. By learning to change their thoughts, clients with these disorders can learn to change their feelings. They learn that they can control their feelings and that they are not victims of their environment. Most people suffering from problems with depression, anxiety, or anger feel that they are depressed, anxious or angry because of the events happening to them. Cognitive therapy can help such individuals realize that by modifying their thoughts, they can gain some mastery over their feelings and reduce their tendencies to react emotionally with depressive feelings, with anxiety, and with anger. For the reader who wants more information on cognitive therapy I refer them to David Burns' excellent book simply titled *Feeling Good: the New Mood Therapy.*

The changes in thinking and feelings resulting from cognitive therapy last longest if they also lead to changes in actions, particularly to changes in the way that we relate to ourselves and to others. Cognitive therapy can empower a client to make changes because the client learns that they do not have to feel the way that they do.

They can learn to master their feelings so they can experience themselves more positively; this in turn can lead them to change some very significant things in their life. Stated another way, cognitive therapy can increase a client's sense of personal power and thus make it more possible for them to work on the differentiation of their self.

On the other hand, cognitive therapy, like any technique, can also result in a client becoming less likely to make real and lasting changes in their life. This occurs when there are problems in the therapy triangle which are not resolved. Thus a technique with the power to help can become destructive when it is used in the context of a therapy triangle which is stuck. Let's look at an example.

Joe, his wife, and Dr. Hugh Mullin, Cognitive Therapist: Joe is a moderately depressed man of 35 who is highly self-critical and whose wife Marge is highly critical of him. She has been frustrated by his lack of enthusiasm and motivation which he has shown for the past five years. She pressures him to get some professional help for one year before he finally goes to see Dr. Hugh Mullin, a therapist who uses cognitive therapy techniques and has a tendency towards being a "shame and blame" therapist (see Chapter 4). Dr. Mullin is very emotionally invested in cognitive therapy and has a deep belief in it partly because it was helpful to him in overcoming his own chronic tendency to criticize himself too harshly and to feel unrealistically guilty.

When Joe first came in, Dr. Mullin asked him about the way he thought about himself and the world and quickly discovered that this client was highly self-critical and unrealistically guilty about many things. Dr. Mullin told Joe that if he would only change his way of thinking (his "self talk" as it is often called) he would be less depressed. He instructed Joe to keep a diary of his thoughts which led to his depressive feelings. Joe, meanwhile, was quite reluctant about being in therapy at all. He felt forced into it by his wife and he was barely able to conceal his resentment about treatment. His wife had been trying to pressure him to be less depressed and more energetic for years and now he had a therapist who was trying to do the same thing. Joe was a very passive man and went along with the therapy without any outward complaints but he quickly began to resist the efforts of the therapist to help him make changes. He felt ganged up on by his wife and his therapist; it was "two against one", the basic structure of an emotional triangle. He came to see Dr. Mullin regularly but he had often "forgotten" his assignments and never could clearly say what he wanted out of therapy. He was pleasant in therapy but never really understood what he was supposed to do, even though his therapist gave him very clear and (potentially) helpful things to do.

As treatment went on, he resisted the helping efforts of both his therapist and his wife, and they both became more and more frustrated with him.

Dr. Mullin began blaming him for not doing his assignments and not working very hard in therapy. He pressured Joe by telling him that if he would only use the techniques he was being taught, he would be much better off. His wife pressured him by telling him that he wasn't getting any better and that if he were really trying, he should be better by now. The more his therapist and his wife pressured him, the more he felt like a failure. He blamed himself for therapy not going well. In his thinking, his failure as a therapy client was just one more example of how he was a failure in most things in his life. His negative thinking about himself was actually strengthened by this application of cognitive therapy! Because cognitive therapy was used in the midst of a therapy triangle where the therapist and the client's wife were in an unrecognized alliance against the client, therapy made matters worse.

What might a more differentiated therapist have done with this case and how could cognitive therapy actually have been helpful to Joe? First of all, if Dr. Mullin were a more differentiated therapist, he would not have been so emotionally invested in the efficacy of cognitive therapy that he would have pushed it on Joe. He would have recognized early in treatment that the client was not motivated to change and he would have explored in depth with Joe why he was really coming to therapy. When Dr. Mullin discovered that Joe was there only because his wife had threatened divorce if he didn't get help, he would shift the focus of therapy to the relationship between husband and wife. He might invite Marge to come to therapy with Joe so that they could work on the marital issues involved.

By bringing Marge into therapy, Dr. Mullin would be trying to find out what her hope was for Joe's treatment and to see if she might be motivated to make some changes in herself. He would also work very hard in his thinking and in his actions to not take sides. He would be working on being comfortable in his mind with both his original client Joe and with Marge. If he were to listen carefully and non-judgmentally to both Joe and Marge, he might discover who really wanted to do what.

Let's say that in this case the therapist finds out that Joe really does want to feel better about himself but what he first wants is for Marge to get off his back, so that he can then feel better about himself. (Remember: clients come to therapy hoping that someone else will change.) Dr. Mullin would realize that Joe cannot make Marge stop criticizing him so harshly, but Dr. Mullin would begin working on that goal with the client because it is the client's goal. He would begin exploring with Joe how he might do some things to try to get his wife off his case. He might coach Joe to not turn away from his wife's criticisms but to listen closely to them and work on being less reactive to or frightened by them. He might coach his client to tell Marge that her criticisms are understandable and that he has heard them but that it is very difficult for him to try to get better when she criticizes him. The important thing here would be for Joe to take some less anxious stands with his wife rather than running away from her.

Let's say that Joe was somewhat successful in doing this and that it worked somewhat: his wife began to tone down her criticisms a bit and he became less frightened of them. He became a little more comfortable around her and began to feel just a bit better about himself. However, he was still faced with his very negative thoughts about himself. With his home life more at peace and with less pressure put on him by his therapist and his wife, his negative patterns of thinking would come more clearly into focus for him and he could begin to work on those patterns. At this point in treatment, he would be ready to use some cognitive therapy techniques to understand and change his highly self-critical way of thinking. He could now benefit from cognitive therapy because he would be motivated to change his thoughts, because he would be less rebellious towards Marge for insisting that he change, and because his therapist was not siding with his wife against him. He could use those techniques to improve his self image which made it clear to him that he needed to make some further changes in the way he related to his wife and to his rather overbearing and overprotective mother. Cognitive therapy could become an aid to his own process of differentiation.

ANXIETY MANAGEMENT TECHNIQUES

There are many specific techniques which therapists use in working with clients who have problems with anxiety. These techniques combine relaxation training techniques with cognitive techniques to help the client reduce his or her fears. Often these techniques involve gradually exposing the client (either in imagination or in real life) to the particular situations which trigger their anxiety and teaching them to master those fears by staying relaxed and thinking less anxiety-provoking thoughts. Like the cognitive techniques discussed in the previous section, these techniques have been extensively researched and have been shown effective in reducing phobias and other anxiety problems for many, many clients.

When these techniques work, the client realizes that they do not have to be a victim to their anxiety. This change often has a profound effect and can make it possible for the client to work on their own differentiation so that their fears and phobias are much less likely to return and they can live a more satisfying life. On the other hand, these same techniques can be helpful at removing or reducing the power of the client's anxiety symptoms but not bring about lasting change because the client does not deal with the underlying problems in themselves or in their relationships which often fuel their anxiety.

For example, I once treated a woman who had a rather serious fear of driving. Because of her fears, she was unable to drive over a bridge which she needed to be able to cross to get to work by the shortest route. Her phobia had begun when she was driving with her husband to a distant city. It was a stormy night and she was at the wheel as they drove through this unfamiliar city. They were traveling on a freeway which was being repaved; the roadway was narrow and had temporary concrete barriers on both sides. Her husband was very angry with her for the way she was driving and began putting her down and yelling at her to be careful. She became very frightened and pulled off the freeway at the next exit, in tears and furious with her husband. He did not apologize to her but called her a "wimp", took the keys from her, and ordered her back in the car. She did not drive the rest of that trip and remained afraid of and furious with her husband.

When she returned home after the trip, she drove to work the next day as she usually did and as she crossed the bridge, the concrete barriers at the side of the bridge reminded her of the concrete barriers on the freeway in the distant city. She began to get extremely frightened and anxious; her heart was racing, her palms began to sweat and she began to feel dizzy and light-headed. She became even more frightened because she thought that she was going to pass out. She managed to get over the bridge and on to work but she was unable to drive over that bridge for many months. She hoped that her phobia would go away by itself but it did not.

When she came to my office, she explained that she wanted to get rid of her fear. From hearing her talk about her relationships to her husband and to her family of origin, I could see that there were significant unresolved problems with them. She clearly felt dominated by and controlled by her husband and there was a serious rift between her and her mother: although they lived in the same town, they saw each other only a few times per year and then their contact was cool and superficial. She also gave me a very clear message that she did not think that there were any problems in her marriage or with her extended family and she did not need any help in those areas. So we worked on the phobia. Because this was a fairly new phobia (only a few months old) and because it was very focused (she was only afraid of the bridge, nothing else in her life), she was able to make rapid improvement in her phobia using some anxiety management techniques. She soon became able to drive over the bridge and she ended therapy, thanking me for my help.

About two years later, she came back to see me.

She said that the phobia had not returned and that she was having no problems driving over the bridge. She did say, however, that she was having serious marital problems and was considering divorce.

Following the treatment of her phobia, she had gradually become aware of how controlling and verbally abusive her husband was to her and she realized more and more clearly that she did not have to live in a marriage like hers. She had begun being more assertive with her husband and found that they were arguing very frequently. She came to get help for her painful marriage which had helped cause the phobia but which, at the time of the phobia, she was not ready to deal with it. Only two years after her phobia was cleared up did she come to a point where the underlying problem had become a problem for her.

Miranda, her mother, and Sarah Jaffe, Anxiety Management Specialist: Anxiety management strategies have been shown to be very effective for many people but, like all therapeutic techniques, they can also serve to prevent improvement in a person's anxiety symptoms if the therapy triangle within which they are used is stuck. Take the case of a 39 year-old woman named Miranda who came to therapy seeking help for her agoraphobia (the fear of going out in public). Her agoraphobia had developed over 10 years to the point where she was virtually housebound. She would only take very brief trips to the grocery store and then only when she was accompanied by her two small children. Otherwise she stayed home. Her mother would come over every day and bring things to her which she needed and could not get because she would not leave the house by herself. Her mother worried about her daily and often anxiously urged her to get help for her condition, saying she needed to get help or her children would be badly affected by it and she would lose her husband. Miranda was very close to and dependent on her mother and both were very frightened about many things. Finally, her mother prevailed and reluctantly Miranda set up an appointment with Sarah Jaffe, a highly trained therapist who specialized in the treatment of agoraphobia and other anxiety problems. Miranda was extremely frightened by the short trip to the therapist's office and she was nervously sitting on the edge of her chair in the waiting room when she was greeted by Ms Jaffe and welcomed into her office.

Ms Jaffe was very knowledgeable about anxiety management techniques and very skilled in their use with clients but she had a tendency to become impatient with her clients for not making progress soon enough. She felt (correctly) that she had the knowledge to help people out of some very crippling psychological problems and that they really ought to follow her directives if they wanted to get better. If they did not do what she said and make progress quickly, she would take that as a threat to her skill as a therapist and she would either give up on them, scold them for being unmotivated, or she would blame them for "getting something out of" their anxiety.

Miranda did not make very rapid progress. Ms Jaffe gave her tasks to do such as monitoring and studying her thoughts and her anxiety level in various situations and eventually taking very short trips outside the house (other than to the therapist's office) in order to gradually reduce her fears. The client tried hard to comply with the therapist's directives but found that some of them, particularly the brief trips outside the house, were just too terrifying. The therapist could see that the client's mother was "enabling" her daughter by helping her out so much that her daughter did not have much incentive to get over her fears and did not have to learn to live a more independent life.

Ms Jaffe began to blame the two women, frustrated that they were so stuck together that the daughter had to have her mother do everything for her and the mother would not see that by "helping" her daughter she was not being helpful. Ms Jaffe asked the mother to come in with her daughter and she confronted both women pointing out that the mother should not be over at her daughter's house every day and should not bring her things which the daughter could get for herself if she would only make more of an effort to conquer her fears. The therapy triangle was becoming set in concrete: it was mother and daughter against therapist.

Ms Jaffe became more frustrated and confrontive with both mother and daughter and as she did this, the mother and daughter drew closer together against the therapist. Mother began to feel protective of her daughter when they were with the therapist because the therapist would criticize the daughter for her lack of progress. The daughter would feel frightened when the therapist would tell the mother that she needed to "let her daughter grow up" because the daughter did not know if she could survive without her mother being very close to and protective of her. Furthermore, the daughter began to feel like a failure as a therapy client and began to feel that she would never get over her phobia. She began to feel even more like a victim of her fears and had less hope for change than when she started treatment. Mother and daughter both dropped out of treatment with Miranda's fears more powerful than ever in both women's minds.

In the hands of a more differentiated therapist, the

same anxiety management techniques could have been more helpful. The therapist would have needed more patience and would have needed to respect both mother and daughter and their extremely close bond. When both failed to comply with the therapist's directions, the therapist would need to remain calm and respect the long-standing family traditions of which these two women were a part. Anxiety management techniques could be helpful in the context of such a therapy triangle but would only bring about change very slowly because Miranda's agoraphobia served a very important purpose: the strengthening of the bond between mother and daughter.

BEHAVIOR MANAGEMENT TECHNIQUES FOR USE WITH CHILDREN

So far in this book we have focused exclusively on the treatment of problems in adults. In this section, we will focus on a set of techniques to help parents and other caretakers create a more stable, predictable, and consistent environment for children who are having behavioral problems such as hitting other children, screaming at parents, and disobeying reasonable commands given by parents. The most frequently used of these techniques are probably time-outs and token reward systems. We will focus on these two techniques to show how they can be very helpful or destructive depending on the therapy triangle in which they are used. Time-outs are used particularly with young children to eliminate unwanted behavior such as hitting others or disobeying. The procedure used with the young child is usually as follows: every time the child does the unwanted behavior, the child is immediately put in a room or other space where they will be isolated from other people and will have nothing entertaining to do.

They are put there for a very short period of time; a frequently used rule of thumb is one minute for every year of the child's age, so three minutes for three year olds. Often parents are advised to tell the child they must be quiet during the time out and not leave the isolation room or space. If the child makes noise or leaves the space during the designated time period, the time period will be started over again.

Token rewards systems are set up so that the child receives rewards for positive behavior (such as doing household chores) and loses rewards for negative behavior (such as refusing to pick up toys when the parent says to do so). For each behavior to be rewarded, a certain number of points or tokens are awarded to the child. For each negative behavior, the child loses a certain number of points or tokens. (It is important to set this up so that the child does not end up with negative points at the beginning because they will become discouraged and give up on the program.) At the end of each week or other such time period, the points that the child has earned are added up and the child can then select from a list of rewards (either things or privileges) which has been drawn up by the parents in consultation with the child. They can spend their tokens or save them up until the next week for some of the larger rewards on the list. It works very much like the economy in which most adults function every day!

These two techniques have been extensively tested and researched and found to be very effective in modifying young children's behavior. However, for these techniques to be most effective, they have to be used consistently by all caretakers in the home. This means that if both parents are in the home, they both have to support and consistently implement whatever program has been set up. It can mean that other frequent caretakers for the child (such as a day-care provider) may also have to follow the program if it is going to succeed. These techniques are behavior modification for the children but they require the adults who take care of them to modify their behavior! These techniques work best in relatively non-anxious families, with relatively non-anxious parents. Time outs, for example, carried out by harried, angry, overwhelmed parents will be done inconsistently and angrily rather than consistently, calmly, and firmly. Therefore, parents who are unable to use these techniques in the proper manner may need to work on themselves before they can even attempt to use these techniques with any hope of success.

As we have seen with the other techniques we have considered, time-outs and token economies can backfire, making the child's behavior problems worse or at least making them more difficult to change. With child behavior management strategies, the most common therapy triangles are therapist-father-mother and therapist-parent-child. The more anxiety there is in the therapy triangle, the more these potentially helpful techniques can be turned against themselves and can make for a worse situation than when change was first attempted.

Melissa, her husband, Dave, and Dr. Steven Hauser, Child Behavior Specialist: Let's see what happened when a well-intentioned but at times overly helpful therapist, Dr. Steven Hauser, began working with Melissa, a harried and frustrated mother of two young boys, whose older son was in the habit of biting and hitting his younger brother. Melissa and her husband Dave were angry and tense around each other most of the time; occasionally they got into shouting matches in front of the children. Dr. Hauser began treatment by advising Melissa to use time-outs to try to eliminate her older son's hitting and biting. It seemed like a reasonable approach to deal with a quite serious problem. However, early in the therapy it became clear that Melissa's husband Dave thought time-outs were worthless and that only spanking would help the child stop biting and hitting. The mother felt very comfortable with Dr. Hauser and trusted that his advice about the time-outs was sound. She tried to carry out the time-outs at home with predictable resistance from her husband and a great deal of kicking and screaming from her older son. A therapy triangle was formed in which Melissa and her therapist were allied with each other against Melissa's husband. The therapist asked Dave to join them in therapy so they could discuss how to work best with their oldest son.

When Dave grudgingly came to a session with his wife, Dr. Hauser tried to persuade Dave that time-outs would be beneficial to the child. Predictably, Melissa took the therapist's side in the ensuing argument. At that point, Dave became very defensive and angry which heightened the fears of both Dr. Hauser and Melissa, causing them to work even harder to make Dave see the rightness of time-outs.

Not surprisingly, the session ended in tension and frustration on all sides. At the next session (attended only by Melissa), Dr. Hauser heard Melissa's complaints about Dave and was emotionally drawn to the mother's side of the conflict. Melissa returned home, determined to follow through with the time-outs. She did so with some success and her son's behavior improved but only when she was at home with him and her husband was gone.

However, when Dave was home, he would tell his son that he would spank him the next time he hit or bit his brother and said, "I don't care what your mother or her shrink says". This statement confused the child and gave him tacit permission to disobey his mother. His behavior deteriorated and at the next session, Melissa was even more distraught than before. Dr. Hauser asked if she had ever considered divorce and she replied that she had thought about it for the part three years but didn't want to break up the family. A few days later, she told her husband that Dr. Hauser raised the question of divorce. Dave became very angry, told his wife that she should not to return to the therapist and she complied. The family got no further help until five years later when the oldest boy was thirteen and had been caught shop lifting CD's from the local discount store.

Melissa, her husband, Dave, and therapist Maria Ramirez: Let's see what happened when this same family presented the same problem to a less anxious therapist, Maria Ramirez. She handled this case quite differently. First of all, she was able to see that the child's behavioral problem was part of a larger context than just mother and son. Second, as the mother expressed her desperate need to do something which would help her control her son's behavior, Ms Ramirez did not feel a complementary desperate need to do something to fix the son's behavior. She was able to maintain a thoughtful and calm stance toward the mother because she realized that this behavior problem was part of a wider family context and had been going on for years and that it would not be fixed by tomorrow or next week. Ms Ramirez did not ignore or discount the problem of the son biting and hitting his brother. After all, this is a serious problem and it is the reason Melissa came for help.

Some therapists in this situation would say something to Melissa like, "Until you get your marriage gets straightened out, nothing you can do with your son will be helpful." This would only serve to ignore the original problem and discourage the mother, leaving her feeling more hopeless than she was when she first came in. Ms Ramirez worked to maintain a balance, pointing out to Melissa that it would be difficult for her to do anything different in her family while keeping her eye on Melissa's agenda which was to change the child's behavior as soon as possible.

Ms Ramirez suggested that Dave and Melissa come in together to help the therapist assess how willing the father was to participate in any behavior modification program. Dave agreed to come in but in the meeting she met with strong resistance from him because he did not see anything wrong with the way he was handling his son and made it clear that he didn't need any help from a therapist to tell him how to be a good parent. At this point, the therapy triangle was taking shape: mother and therapist against father. The most natural thing for a therapist to do at this point is to explicitly or implicitly side with the mother against the father because the mother is clearly more open to the wisdom which the therapist has to offer. This is a trap. Ms Ramirez saw that this triangle was developing and decided not to challenge the father but simply to accept his point of view. She decided to let him be at this point; she did not protest or argue when, at the end of the session, he said he would never come back. She continued to work with the mother with an understanding and acceptance of the fact that the father would be impeding any implementation of a behavioral program for the child. It was very difficult for Ms Ramirez (as it is for most therapists) to be at peace with the reality that there are people who will neither listen to nor follow their advice, particularly when the therapist is sure that the advice they have to offer would make their clients' lives better!

As the weeks passed, Ms Ramirez worked with Melissa to use time outs with the child while being aware of the mother's limitation to effect change because her husband was not invested in the project. She also helped Melissa to deal with the triangle she was in at home, the triangle involving herself, her husband, and her son. She coached Melissa to be very clear with both her husband and her son about her limitations: Melissa began saying things to her husband like, "I'm going to be using time outs with Chad whenever he bites Joey. I realize that you are not going to use this same way of dealing with him but I feel that it is what I need to do. I'd like to explain to you exactly what I'm going to do next time Chad bites Joey just so that you'll know. But I realize you have your own ways of handling this same situation. I'd like you to use time-outs but I can't force you to."

She might say to her son something like, "Chad, I'm going to be doing something different from now on when-ever you bite or hit your brother. I'll take you into the bath-room, close the door and leave you there for three minutes. I'll set the timer and when it rings you can come out. When dad is with you, I think he'll handle things differently but I'm just telling you what I'm going to do." In order for Melissa to make these statements and stick to them, she needed to become surer of herself with both her son and her husband. When she had some success with Chad's behavior (which she did, even though her husband contin-ued to spank and yell) her confidence as a mother went up. Her expectations that her husband would change were lowered and in this way the small gains that she did make were more meaningful to her and she will saw them as a partial success rather than a complete failure. Melissa continued to use the time-outs firmly and confidently, and she achieved more success in controlling her son's behavior. As a result, she felt less overwhelmed and she was freer to deal with difficulties in her marriage and in other areas of her life. A relatively non-anxious therapist like Maria Ramirez can use the behavioral technique of time-outs to promote the differentiation of the mother (who is the one in the family motivated to change) and to reduce the problem behavior of the child which was the client's original purpose for therapy. The same technique in the hands of a reactive and overly helpful therapist, like Dr. Hauser, will lead to discouragement and a sense of failure on the part of the mother, no change on the part of the child, and increased anger on the part of the father.

PSYCHIATRIC MEDICATION

Medication, like the psychotherapy techniques described previously, can be helpful and even essential in helping some clients to make lasting changes. By reducing clients' symptoms, and by increasing the control that the client has over his or her thoughts, behaviors, and emotions, the client's sense of personal empowerment can increase. There has been an explosion of interest in psychiatric medication in recent years largely because of newly developed drugs such as the Prozac family of medications which are used primarily to treat depression and anxiety disorders. There are also medications for the treatment of attention deficit disorder, bi-polar disorder (formerly known as manic-depression), schizophrenia, obsessive-compulsive disorder, and many other disorders. For many of these conditions, the use of psychiatric medication is essential for the client to get better; for others it is helpful but not essential. It is far beyond the scope of both my expertise and this book to discuss which medications are used to treat which disorders and in what cases medication is essential for the client to make progress. What I want to focus on is how medication fits into the therapy triangle and how the dynamics in that triangle influence its long-term effectiveness.

To begin, I want to point out that clients who are prescribed medication for their disorder are often told by their psychiatrist (or family doctor) that they have a "chemical imbalance" which is genetic in origin and essentially unrelated to how they are living their lives, what they are thinking, their relationships with others, or their work. The doctor implies that once they get the right medication in the right dosage, once the problem with their brain chemistry is cleared up, then their problems will disappear.

The psychiatrist implies that they do not need to seek help for their relationships or their ways of thinking and behaving; he or she implies that those problems are completely caused by the chemical problems in the client's brain. This approach to medication and mental disorders appears to be based on the following idea: a person's brain chemistry causes thoughts, behaviors, and feelings but their thoughts, behaviors, and feelings have little or no effect on brain chemistry. There is, as you might expect, plenty of evidence which supports the idea that brain chemistry affects thoughts, feelings, and behaviors. It is easy to observe this by watching someone get drunk or high on drugs. The drug influences their brain chemistry which leads to changes in their thoughts, feelings, and behaviors.

There is also plenty of evidence which supports the

idea that the way people think, feel, and behave influences their neuro-chemistry. This is harder to observe in every day life because no one can observe (without special equipment) their own or someone else's brain chemistry! However, if you have ever been frightened walking down a darken street you will see that your behavior (walking down the street) coupled with your thoughts ("somebody might be waiting to mug me around the corner of that building") will cause a big change in your brain chemistry which will send signals to your adrenal glands to release large amounts of adrenaline which causes your heart to pound, your body to sweat, and your mind to achieve a hyper-alert status called fear. Your brain chemistry would not be what it is if you were not walking down the street thinking those frightening thoughts! I am drastically simplifying a vast area of research but I would propose a model of understanding the relationship between thoughts, behaviors, and feelings on the one hand and brain chemistry on the other: the two sides influence each other in a circular way as depicted in Figure 6.

FIGURE 6

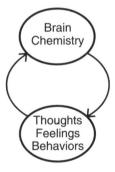

The point of this diagram is that each side influences the other.

The important implications for a discussion of psychiatric medication are that a change in brain chemistry (such as by taking medication) can change thoughts, feelings, and behaviors and that changes in thoughts, feelings, and behaviors (such as changes brought about through psychotherapy) can make changes in brain chemistry. Thus some depressed people whose brain chemistry is serving to maintain their depression can be helped by psychotherapy without medication because the changes they make in therapy (such as learning to think more positively, being more assertive with others) can influence their brain chemistry in ways which will make their brain less "depressed"! I am not saying that all cases of depression can be cured without medication; clinical experience and research show us that this is not the case. However, Figure 6 does show how changing brain chemistry (through medication) and changing the psychological factors (through psychotherapy) can work together to help a client get better and that intervening in either brain chemistry or psychological factors can positively influence the other side. With this concept as background, let's look further into how psychiatric medication can be helpful or harmful, depending on how the therapy triangle is managed.

Barbara, Her Abusive Husband, and Dr. Stanley Gunther, Psychiatrist: Consider the case of Dr. Stanley Gunther, a rather rigid and dogmatic psychiatrist who is convinced that medication is the only effective treatment for depression. In this case, we will see how Dr. Gunther's treatment can inadvertently reinforce and strengthen a patient's depression even when he is prescribing the correct medication at the correct dosage.

Here's how this can work: A seriously depressed 35

year-old woman named Barbara Luciano comes to see Dr. Gunther. Barbara has been married since age 18 to a man who has verbally abused her throughout their marriage and who has physically abused her on numerous occasions. She was well prepared for this type of relationship by being verbally and physically abused by her older brothers. Dr. Gunther is very competent technically in that he is skilled at diagnosing patients and skilled at knowing the right medication and the right dosages to prescribe to his patients. He is dogmatic in that he believes that depression is purely a "chemical imbalance" which can only be treated by medication. He interviews Barbara carefully but is very selective about what he focuses on: he notes carefully the signs and symptoms of her depression such as her low mood, her frequent crying spells, her difficulties sleeping and eating, her lack of motivation and thoughts of suicide.

When he discovers that her husband is abusive to her and that her current episode of depression began six months ago when her husband got laid off from his job and began drinking more heavily, he downplays the importance of this information.

At the end of the interview, he tells her that she has a "chemical imbalance" and that her relationship with her husband has nothing to do with her depression. He hands her a prescription for anti-depressant medication, carefully gives her instructions on how to take the mediation, and schedules a time to see her again in one month.

When she arrives home, her husband asks her what the "shrink" had to say about her. She tells him that he said she has a chemical problem in her brain and that the medication he gave her should clear things up. Barbara, like many women who are abused and like many people who are depressed, blames herself for any problems which occur in her vicinity; she now blames herself for being depressed. Her belief that she is the problem is strengthened by Dr. Gunther's statement that her problem is in her brain. One of the cornerstones of her depression, her belief that she is inadequate, defective, and to blame is strengthened.

Her husband has been blaming her for years for the problems between the two of them. He has sought to control her by degrading her both physically and verbally and he has been quite successful. When he hears that she is the problem, he is greatly relieved because he was afraid she was going to wind up with a "shrink" who would tell her that he is the problem. One of his core beliefs, that she is weak, defective, and to blame for their troubles, is also strengthened. An unspoken and unrecognized alliance between the husband and the psychiatrist against the patient is being formed.

When the patient returns to the psychiatrist a month later, she is feeling better. The medication has worked well for her and she is feeling a bit more positive and more motivated than before. She is less moody and irritable around her husband, which her husband appreciates. The doctor is pleased with her progress, makes a minor modification in her dosage, and schedules to see her in another month. She is feeling somewhat better and she decides that she will start spending one evening per week with her female friends, talking and having dinner, a habit which she had stopped six months earlier when she had gotten so depressed. To her husband, the sight of her (relatively) happily going out with her friends for an evening is very threatening. He feels that her friends, some of whom have been divorced, might fill her head with ideas about what a jerk he is and how she should leave him. He becomes very irritable and angry as she prepares to go out and tells her darkly that he is not sure where he will be when she gets home.

After she leaves, he begins drinking heavily so that by the time she arrives home at 11:00, he is quite drunk. He begins calling her a slut and a whore and smacks her across the face. She is devastated as she realizes that her beatings have started up again. She gets a nasty black eye from the blow and calls in sick to work the next day because she can't cover up the black eye successfully with make up.

She stays home from work for four days and her self esteem (which was propped up greatly by her competence in her job) begins to go down again. Her husband threatens to beat her worse if she goes out again with her female friends and she begins to sink lower still.

When she returns to see the psychiatrist for her next appointment, her black eye has healed but she is nearly as depressed as she was when she first came to see him. She has been taking her medication faithfully according to his instructions and yet she is no better off. At that point, her psychiatrist changes her to a different medication which causes some uncomfortable side effects but still helps some with her mood. After a few weeks she decides that treatment is not being helpful to her so she stops taking her medication and cancels her next appointment with Dr. Gunther. She is more convinced than ever that she is "bad" and that she will never get better because even the best medication could not help her. She goes on being abused and put down by her husband and sinks deeper and deeper into depression.

The moral of this story is that even the best medication taken diligently by a motivated patient can result in a long-term negative outcome. Barbara got worse because she got better. Her improvement in mood led her to act more independently with her husband, which threatened him greatly and led to him abusing her. His abuse resulted in her feeling more depressed and more helpless about herself than she had when she came to treatment. When a strong and completely unrecognized triangle develops such as the one between Dr. Gunther, Barbara, and her husband, the best medication may be of no help in the long run. Barbara did experience some improvement on the medication; it was effective in lessening her depressive symptoms. If she could have been guided to use her improved mood to work on some of the very difficult problems in her family life, she could have made lasting changes. But the therapy triangle remained unrecognized by all parties and was never made part of the treatment. The traditions which Barbara and her husband carried from their families, traditions of physically abusive men and intimidated, depressed women proved to be stronger than the medication.

A psychiatrist who was less dogmatic than Dr. Gunther would have recognized more clearly how this woman's depression was tied to her abusive marriage and to her family traditions. He or she would have realized that unless there were some changes in the way she dealt with herself and her husband, her depression would win out. If the psychiatrist were not trained as a therapist, he or she could have referred her to a therapist, hopefully to a well-differentiated one. The therapist could have helped her to see how her depression was a part of a very painful family situation and could have helped her to make some changes in herself so that she would not tolerate the abuse.

In that case, the initial, short-term benefit which she received from the medication would have helped empower her to increase her level of differentiation. The medication and the psychotherapy would have worked together and the outcome of treatment would have been significantly better.

Pearl of Wisdom: There are many therapeutic techniques and many psychiatric medications which can help to reduce the power of your symptoms and help you feel more in control of your life. In the long run, these improvements in your symptoms can lead either to lasting change or, ironically, to maintaining or even worsening your problems. Only if the reduction in symptoms leads you to increase your level of differentiation will you make lasting changes. It is that simple and that difficult.

Chapter 8

Some Questions of Logistics

Up to this point, we have focused on the big issues in therapy, particularly how the therapy triangle has such a powerful impact on the success or failure of treatment. This book would not be complete, however, if we did not spend some time on the smaller, more practical questions about therapy. So, in this second to last chapter, I will answer six questions which are frequently asked by clients and prospective clients. Hopefully, the answers will help you figure out how you can work with a helpful therapist over a significant enough period of time so that you can make the changes you want.

QUESTION 1:
HOW DO I DECIDE IF I SHOULD
GO TO THERAPY OR NOT?

The short answer to this question is simple: go to therapy when you feel stuck. When you or someone close to you has been struggling with a problem in thinking, feeling, or behavior for a month or more, then you can use professional help. When the problem keeps coming back or never leaves despite your best efforts to solve it, then you can use help. Notice that I said that you should seek help if you or someone close to you has a problem. You may feel that you are doing well in your life but that your child, your spouse, your mother, your father, your siblings, or your closest friend is having a significant problem and they seem stuck in it. Of course you can recommend that they seek help but that recommendation may fall on deaf ears.

My recommendation to you is to *seek help for your-self even when you do not think you are the one with the problem.* Time and energy expended on urging a reluctant family member or friend into treatment is not time well spent. Going for help yourself is a much better investment, particularly if you are able to raise your level of differenti-ation as we discussed in a previous chapter. If you raise your own level of differentiation, then the family member or friend who "has the problem" may feel more motivated to solve it. But there are no guarantees.

One of the most difficult parts of making the deci-sion to get professional help is overcoming a sense of shame or failure. There still exists in most of our minds a stigma against seeking out professional help. Many people have the idea that to seek professional help is a sign of weakness, craziness, or both.

Many of us will say that we don't believe that, but when it comes down to making the decision to get help for oneself or one's family, the sense of shame and failure comes to the forefront of our minds and we begin to resist the idea of seeking help. Overcoming your resistance to getting help can be difficult and prolonged. Often people consider therapy for years before actually seeking it out. Not until a crisis in their lives increases their level of psy-chological pain will their resistance to seeking help be overcome.

This leads me to a piece of tongue-in-cheek advice: if you are stuck in a problem and you could benefit from professional help but you are resisting going to therapy for one reason or another, arrange to have a crisis in your life. Make a bad decision in a relationship, blow up at your child, bring yourself to the brink of being fired at work, or do something else which will get you to a point of fear and desperation, to a point where you are convinced that you cannot solve your problems on your own. Your crisis will help convince you that now is the time to seek help. Pain can help you clarify our need for help. If you are in a lot of pain and have experienced a crisis, you can be (grudgingly) thankful for your pain because it can help you decide to get the help you may have needed for quite some time. When you are in pain, take the opportunity which it presents to make the changes which will make your life better.

One further word: if you are not sure that you need professional help but want a professional opinion about whether or not you could benefit from it, go to a therapist who can give you an evaluation. In a few sessions (perhaps aided by some psychological testing or a consultation with a psychiatrist), a competent professional can give you an idea of whether or not you need help and, if so, what are the major issues you need to work on at this time. An evaluation like this can help you find out more about yourself and your struggles without committing you to therapy. Beware, however, of having a poorly differentiated professional do this evaluation. Abusive therapists will try to frighten and coerce you into treatment, shame-and-blame therapists will blame you or your "other" or both, overly helpful therapists will anxiously nurture you into therapy and a withdrawn therapist will not give you much useful information at all.

QUESTION 2:
WHO SHOULD GO TO THERAPY WITH ME?

This question is particularly addressed to the person who worries that a family member has a problem but sees him- or herself as reasonably problem-free. Parents worried about children, partners and spouses worried about their mates, and adult children worried about their parents are probably the most common examples of these situations. In these cases, the person who sees the problem in the other person is tempted to try to force that person into treatment.

Often in cases which are seen by the clients as marital problems, both partners believe that the other person is the only one with a problem. Often with marital problems, one partner is more motivated than the other to make changes in themselves.

My rule of thumb in these situations is that only the people who are willing to go to therapy should go. Twisting someone's arm to go into therapy is almost always counter-productive. As a result of the arm-twisting, they may get to therapy but they are likely to be so resistant to the process that they get very little out of it. In fact, the whole experience may convince them even further that therapy is a waste of time because they are dedicated to defeating the process. People who believe that therapy is a waste of time usually turn out to be right!

Remember what we discussed in Chapter 2: in order to be motivated for therapy, clients must be in pain and have a sense of responsibility for doing something to solve their problems. So, if you are concerned about someone close to you who has a problem which you think could benefit from professional help but they don't think so, go for help yourself. You can benefit from the help because you want to benefit from it. Granted, you don't have the problem but, if you find a good therapist, you may learn how you might contribute to maintaining the problem. From there, you can learn to work on your own level of differentiation so that you stop unintentionally helping to maintain the problem. You may even find that by changing yourself and contributing less to the maintenance of the problem, the person with the problem will find him- or herself in more pain and then he or she may want to do something to resolve the problem.

In order to clarify and illustrate these ideas, I'd like to discuss two of the common situations in which the person who is motivated to get help is not the person who "has" the problem: parents concerned about problems in their minor children and spouses (or other intimate partners) concerned about problems in their partner. First, let's look at how children and adolescents fit into therapy. Pre-adolescent children are almost never motivated to make changes in themselves. They may have very serious problems which need attention from others to solve but they are very rarely motivated to do something to change the way they are. They may have the problem but they are rarely willing and able (by themselves) to come up with the solution. Teenagers also are very rarely motivated to make changes in themselves in treatment. They are often strongly motivated to have the adults in their lives make changes but only rarely are they willing to make changes in themselves. Those few adolescents interested in making changes in themselves tend to be older adolescents (ages 17-19).

So what should you do if you see your child having serious problems? It may be very helpful at the beginning to have your child or adolescent come in a few times to see a professional to evaluate the child and to try to understand their point of view about the problem. This evaluation may or may not include testing by a psychologist or examination by a psychiatrist. A competent assessment of your child can make it more possible for the therapist to help you help your child. Like many parents bringing their child for help, you may expect that the therapist will make your child better. But remember, your child or adolescent will rarely make changes in themselves because they are rarely motivated to do so. Almost always, changes in your child will come from changes in their environment. And the most powerful part of their environment is you, their parent.

After your child has been evaluated and both you and your therapist feel that you have an understanding of what needs to be done to help your child get better, then you and any others close to your child who are motivated should go for help to make changes in your selves which will benefit your child. The changes in your child will need to come from you and from others who are concerned, not from your child. Many parents bring their children to therapists so that the professional can "fix" the child; this rarely works. Nevertheless, parents (and some therapists) unwisely invest much time and money into "fixing" children who don't want professional help but invest little time and money into helping those who are motivated to use professional help to make significant changes.

Nora, the protagonist in our extended therapy story, faced a problem with her son Quinn which illustrates some of these ideas. As you may remember, Quinn had a serious case of asthma which he was not taking care of responsibly. He was also getting very poor grades in college and generally not taking responsibility for himself. Nora discovered in therapy that she was taking too much responsibility for Quinn in many aspects of his life and that by her taking too much responsibility for him, she was contributing to Quinn's not taking responsibility for himself. We saw that as Nora's therapy proceeded, she took less and less responsibility for him. As she did this, he eventually learned to take more responsibility for himself. But remember, this was a difficult and painful struggle for Nora and did not result in steady, "straight- line" changes in Quinn. He got worse (being hospitalized for his asthma and flunking out of college) before he got better. He got better, not because he went to therapy (he didn't see the need), but because his mother made some changes in the way she was with him. She was the one motivated to make changes.

Now let's look at what happens in marriages and other intimate partnerships when only one of the partners is willing to seek professional help for problems in their partner or in the relationship. Usually the one who is motivated to seek help is in more pain than their partner and has a stronger sense of responsibility for doing something about the problem. The one who is motivated for help then considers their options: Should I demand that my partner go for treatment by herself? Should I force my partner to come to treatment with me? Should I do nothing and watch the problem get worse? Or, should my partner go to treatment by herself?

If your partner is unwilling to go for help, I recommend that you go to treatment by yourself. If your partner is reluctant but willing to go for help, then invite but do not pressure your partner to go to therapy with you. If your partner is reluctant about therapy, don't be surprised if your partner gets nothing out of therapy and drops out after a few sessions. Remember, if you make some changes that will put pressure on the other member of that partnership to change.

Nora faced this problem in her treatment and in her struggle towards health. When her treatment began, she was aware that there were rather serious problems in her marriage. She was overwhelmed by her own anxiety symptoms and, thanks to the pain caused by her anxiety, she entered therapy without waiting to persuade Charlie to come to therapy with her. As she got her anxiety symptoms under control, she began to work on her relationship with Charlie. She worked hard to make changes in the way she was with him and also worked very hard to let go of Charlie and stop trying to change him. These changes in her led in the short run to increased difficulties in their relationship, increased pain on Charlie's part and, eventually to increased motivation on Charlie's part to make changes in the way he was with Nora. Charlie and Nora eventually saw Dr. Kleinfelter together and did some significant work on their relationship making it much more satisfying for both of them. Of course, things do not work so well for many partnerships. Even if the person in Nora's position increases her level of differentiation, the person in Charlie's position may continue to refuse to make any changes and this may lead to stagnation and frustration in the relationship and at times to the dissolution of the partnership.

QUESTION 3:
HOW CAN YOU FIND A THERAPIST
WHO WILL BE HELPFUL TO YOU?

The process of finding a helpful therapist can be broken down into two tasks: first, using information from others to generate a list of a few potential therapists who might be able to help you and, second, using your own perceptions in the first session or two with a therapist on your list to evaluate them (while they are evaluating you!). Coming up with a list of potential therapists is usually done using information about the therapist from four sources: former or current clients, other helping professionals, advertising, and lists of therapists who are approved by your insurance company.

Some of the most helpful opinions about a therapist can be given to you by a friend or relative who has been significantly helped by a particular therapist. A positive recommendation from a former client whom you know and respect does not guarantee that this therapist will be helpful to you, but it is a good sign. If you are lucky enough to have two or three friends or relatives you respect give positive testimonials about the same therapist, then you have even stronger evidence.

Another source of information about therapists is from helping professionals who often refer people for therapy. Physicians and other medical personnel, clergy people, employee assistance counselors, and other therapists are all potentially good sources of information about therapists in your area. When one of these helping professionals recommends a therapist to you, ask them what they know about this therapist, how many people they have referred to them, and what those clients have told them about therapy after the referral. For example, if your minister refers you to Dr. Elizabeth Johanssen, ask your minister how many people he or she has referred to Dr. Johanssen and what those people have told the minister about their therapy. Obviously, the minister will not be able to reveal any details about the treatment because of confidentiality but he or she can give you a general sense of the client's opinion of Dr. Johanssen. The more information you can get directly or indirectly from people who have been treated by a particular therapist, the better off you are. This is because therapy is a very private art; generally no one sees a therapist at work except his or her clients. Also, quality is very hard to assess. Someone may be very impressed by a therapist's credentials and training and refer you to them without knowing much from clients who have worked with that therapist.

You can also glean some information about therapists in the Yellow Pages or other similar advertising. This information should be taken with many grains of salt. A therapist may be able to create (or pay someone to create) an attractive ad but this does not mean that they are competent therapists!

It may be that the therapists with the best ads are the worst therapists because they have to overcome their inadequate skills and their poor reputations! This is certainly not always true but I recommend looking at therapist ads very skeptically particularly if you have no other information about a particular therapist. If their ads sound too good to be true they no doubt are!

Generating a list of therapists must take into account whether you can afford their services or not. Finding out what their hourly fees are may not tell you whether you can afford them or not because your health insurance (if you are fortunate enough to have it) may pay a portion of the cost. You need to find out what the cost of each therapist will be to you. More and more insurance plans will only cover the services of therapists with whom they have a contract. Your insurance carrier should have a list of such therapists.

The best way to find out about your coverage if you have some kind of insurance (after you have tried and failed to decipher the material which the insurance company provides to you), is to call your insurance company and ask what coverage your policy has for outpatient treatment of "nervous and mental disorders" and if there are any restrictions on what therapists are covered by your plan (and therefore which ones are not). You can also call the therapists on your list and ask them if they are eligible to be reimbursed by your insurance company. The phrase "nervous and mental disorders" is important because that is what insurance companies generally call psychiatric or psychological disorders. If you ask your insurance company what coverage there is in your policy for "marital problems" or "relationship problems" they will almost invariably tell you there is no coverage. This is because marital problems are not a medically diagnosable condition. Dr. Kleinfelter appropriately submitted claims to Nora's insurance company indicating that Nora was diagnosed and being treated for an anxiety disorder. Dr. K. knew that she was treating Nora's anxiety disorder partially by treating her relationship problems with her husband, her son, and her parents.

Let's imagine now that you have come up with a list of four therapists who have been recommended to you by respected friends, relatives, helping professionals and your insurance company. How do you go about evaluating these professionals to try to determine whether they can be helpful to you or not?

The best time to evaluate a potential therapist is in the first few sessions you spend with them, although they can also be evaluated in a phone call. It is important that you get to know their training and credentials, their experience and knowledge of your particular problem, and how long they have been in practice. It is most important, of course, to get a sense of how differentiated the therapist is.

Level of differentiation is more difficult to assess than their credentials and their experience but it is more important, as we saw earlier in this book. As you spend time with your therapist, listen to the words they say but also watch how they handle themselves. It will be difficult to consciously observe your therapist in the session because you will be busy with other things: explaining your difficulties, giving your personal history, and explaining what you would like to get out of therapy.

If you are like many clients, you will be in a great deal of emotional distress and this will make it particularly difficult to evaluate how differentiated your therapist is! What would probably be most helpful is to think through by yourself after the session to what degree your therapist seems to embody the characteristics of a relatively well-differentiated person: being able to think and not just react, possessing a sense of inner peace and security, and having the ability to connect with others without trying to control them.

This leads me to suggest that you ask yourself the following questions about a therapist after you have seen them once or twice:

1. Did she seem to be listening carefully to and thinking about what I was saying?

2. Was she able to speak knowledgeably about my problems and about therapy without acting like she knew all the answers?

3. Did she seem at ease during the interview or did she seem insecure or afraid?

4. Did she seem to listen to me without judging or without "pushing" me into doing or thinking the "right" or "healthy" thing?

5. Did she give advice or her opinion too quickly? Or, conversely, did she completely refuse to give any advice or opinions?

6. Was she willing and able to collaborate with me to set the goals of treatment or did she seem to be pushing me to adopt her goals?

7. Was she willing and able to work with me to determine the type of treatment I would receive or did she seem to be pushing me to follow her type of treatment even if I objected?

If the answers to these questions lead you to believe that she is a relatively well-differentiated therapist, then you may be in luck. If she is both well differentiated and knowledgeable about your type of problem, then you have done very well.

No matter how well you evaluate the therapist with whom you start, you may find later that your therapist is not being very helpful to you or even harmful to you. If that happens, you may need to read the answer to the next question.

QUESTION 4:
HOW DO YOU KNOW
IF YOU SHOULD CHANGE THERAPISTS?

If by the end of the third session you do not have a clearer understanding of your problems and a sense of hope that you can do something about your problems which will help you feel better, you should consider changing therapists. This is a rather dogmatic statement which certainly is not true for all therapist/client relationships, but there is research that shows that your probability of positive change goes up significantly if by the third session you have increased both your understanding of your difficulties and your hope of getting better. Some people are in such pain and have been in intense pain for so long that they do not increase their understanding and hope after a few sessions but for most clients, this three-session rule is a good rule of thumb.

If you have made no significant changes by the 10th session, then it is important to reassess your therapy relationship. I am not talking here about solving your problems by the 10th session but about making some improvement in the problems which brought you to therapy in the first place. If you have seen no improvement in ten sessions (and certainly if you have gone backwards in that time), then you might consider the following three possibilities:

1. You need medication or a change in medication. If you believe that you need medication, talk to your therapist and get a referral to a psychiatrist or other physician who can prescribe medication for you (and re-read the section on medication in Chapter 7).

2. You are working with a relatively undifferentiated therapist. If you believe that you are working with a therapist who is one of the types of unhelpful therapists described in Chapter 4 (abusive, shame-and-blame, overly helpful, or withdrawn) then change therapists (and return to Question 3 in this chapter).

3. You are stuck in a problematic therapy triangle. If you believe that you don't need medication (and neither does your therapist) and that your therapist is not only competent but also reasonably well differentiated, then you are not making progress because you are stuck in a difficult therapy triangle. It is time to re-think your therapy efforts. Re-read Chapter 5 and think carefully about yourself, your "others" and your therapist. Consider whether or not you are spending your efforts trying to change your "other" rather than changing yourself. Write down your thoughts and bring them to your therapist for his or her input. He or she may be able to shed some light on how you are stuck and, if you can redirect your efforts towards changing yourself (which is possible) and away from changing others (which is impossible) then you may be able to make some significant and lasting changes.

QUESTION 5:
HOW LONG SHOULD YOU STAY IN THERAPY
IN ORDER TO MAKE LASTING CHANGES?

I have seen clients make important and lasting changes in one or two sessions and I have seen clients who have taken hundreds of sessions over many years to make significant and lasting changes. With this huge range, it makes it very difficult to set a certain number for all clients.

Another factor in answering this question is that therapy is practiced (or used by clients) differently than it used to be. Therapy was originally taught and practiced by psychoanalysts who believed that the client should stay in therapy until their symptoms and the underlying psychological problems which caused those symptoms were completely resolved. The analyst was taught to pressure clients into staying in analysis until they were cured, in the judgment of the analyst. Today, clients come to therapy to work on a particular problem for a relatively short period of time; when therapy is successful, they tend to leave therapy when that problem is resolved to their satisfaction.

Often, the client returns to therapy with the same therapist or a different one at a later point in their life. They may be struggling with a recurrence of their original problem or be dealing with an essentially new one. They will work on this problem for some time in therapy, then end therapy but return again at a later time.

In traditional psychoanalysis, these brief treatment episodes throughout a person's life are seen as failures because therapy is supposed be a long, uninterrupted treatment resulting in the cure of the patient. However, in most forms of therapy as they are practiced today, brief treatment episodes throughout a client's life are seen by professionals as a very successful form of therapy. This style of practice is less costly than the traditional style and so it fits well with the pressure on therapists to keep costs low.

Given that therapy is generally much briefer than it used to be, how can you stay in therapy long enough to make sure your changes last? Here are some guidelines which apply to many, but not all therapy clients:

1. At the beginning of therapy, if you are in a great deal of pain brought on by a crisis in your life, see your therapist frequently, somewhere between once a week and twice a month until you have begun to reduce your level of pain and have begun to make some significant changes in your life.

2. When you begin to feel more comfortable with the changes you have made and they begin to feel "natural" rather than foreign to you, reduce the frequency of your sessions to between once a month and once every two months. Use those sessions to work on your level of differentiation in your relationships: work on defining yourself and connecting non-anxiously with your family of origin, your current family, your work system and your friends. This will strengthen your psychological immune system.

3. Once you have done significant work which has helped raise your level of differentiation, keep seeing your therapist periodically for another year or so. You may only need to be seen every two to six months to keep yourself focused on your level of differentiation.

4. After ending therapy, if you run into other problems and feel stuck, do not hesitate to return to therapy. Your pain may be pushing you to grow more!

5. More important than these guidelines is the ability of you and your therapist to negotiate the frequency of sessions between the two of you. Remember, therapy is supposed to be a collaborative relationship!

QUESTION 6:
HOW CAN YOU AFFORD THERAPY?

Obviously, the answer to this question depends to some degree on how much money you have and how good your insurance coverage is. If you are wealthy or you have generous and unrestricted insurance coverage (or both), then the affordability of therapy is not an issue. For everyone else, this is a difficult and important issue.

The less money you have and the poorer your insurance benefits are for therapy, the more you will need to persist and to advocate for yourself to get the help you need. The fewer resources you have, the more assertive you will have to be to get the help you need; unfortunately, many clients are coming to therapy because it has been difficult for them to be assertive and take charge of their lives! Catch-22!

If you are struggling to survive financially and have no health insurance for psychotherapy, the issue of the affordability of therapy is particularly acute. You might be directed to a public facility such as a community mental health center. At these facilities, professionals are not paid as much as they are elsewhere and their workloads are often very high. As a result, a significant number of the therapists working at such facilities are either inexperienced or overloaded or both. There is also often a cumbersome bureaucracy which you have to deal with just to be seen. You may need to work very hard and be very persistent to find a therapist who can be genuinely helpful to you within that system.

It is important to remember that even if you have little or no money or insurance coverage, you do have options other than your county mental health system. If you are a veteran, the Veteran's Administration runs outpatient clinics (but you may find the same difficulties that you found at the state or county agency). In most cities, there are non-profit agencies which will see clients on a sliding scale basis with your fee per session determined by your income. These agencies are often supported by the United Way or other charitable organizations. These agencies can be a good source of low-cost and competent help. You will need to be persistent and keep looking there for a therapist who can be helpful to you. Another option if you have limited funds is to go to a training clinic run by a university. Most major universities have training programs for psychiatrists, psychologists, social workers, and counselors and, in order to get training for their trainees, they run clinics and treat people for fees determined by their income. Because these are training clinics, you will be seeing an inexperienced therapist but some inexperienced therapists (if they are well differentiated!) can be excellent and genuinely helpful to you.

Another group of people for whom the affordability of therapy is an issue is those with managed care insurance. Some of these plans are excellent and provide generous benefits and at least some choice of therapists at very little out-of-pocket cost to the client. Other plans are very restrictive, giving you little choice of therapist and paying for only a very few sessions because they want to reduce the cost of therapy by offering as little of it as possible.

I once saw a young woman with just such insurance who was seriously depressed, was cut off from her abusive and alcoholic family and who was going through a divorce, raising a one-year old child by herself and had a prescription drug abuse problem. The insurance company authorized four sessions to complete her treatment! An obviously impossible task. Needless to say she had no money to pay for treatment on her own.

To deal with managed care plans, you may need to be a very strong advocate for yourself and find a therapist who will go to bat for you. Some companies are very difficult to deal with and others are more flexible.

If your company is inflexible and provides inadequate treatment, make that known to your employer or your union or choose a different insurance option if you can at your next enrollment period. Also, remember that you may have options other than those given by your insurance company. You can try the sliding scale agencies and clinics as if you had no insurance. If you are seeing a therapist whose services are reimbursed by your insurance but that reimbursement is ended after an inadequate number of sessions and you can't get the company to authorize more sessions, then negotiate with your therapist. Perhaps he or she will continue to see you at a reduced rate and you can reduce the frequency of your sessions to make it possible for you to afford therapy.

Pearl of Wisdom: Logistical problems such as finding a good therapist, deciding who should go to therapy, deciding when to change therapists, deciding how long to stay in therapy and figuring out how you can afford therapy can prevent you from making lasting changes. However, you can often overcome such logistical problems with persistence and self-assertion. If you are blaming the failure of your therapy on logistical problems, think creatively about ways to get around those problems. Logistical problems often get inaccurately blamed for the failure of therapy.

Empowering you with the knowledge to heal

Chapter 9

A String of Pearls and a Farewell

My work as the author of this book is almost done but I presume that your work as a therapy client has a ways to go. My mission has been to present to you the therapy triangle: how it can help you and how it can hurt you. I hope that your understanding of the web that is woven between you, your therapist, and your family will empower you to make important and lasting changes in your life.

My only job left is to provide you with a summary of the ideas in this book by stringing together some of the "pearls of wisdom" with which I have ended each chapter. I present them with a slightly different spin than I did in the body of the book.

Before you begin therapy, make sure you are in psychological pain and that you feel responsible for doing something about that pain. Why would a therapist who is in the business of helping people live more satisfying and less painful lives recommend psychological pain? Because unless you are in pain and feel responsible for doing something about that pain, you will not be motivated to make the difficult changes required to create a better life for yourself. Usually you will need a crisis to make the pain in your life worse and bring into sharp focus your need to do something different. If you are ready for therapy, you will have already had some sort of crisis which has enabled you to take the difficult step of getting help. If you have been in therapy for a while, you might also have the sense that you are responsible for doing something to make things different. If you didn't feel responsible, you would not be reading this book, seeking out a therapist, or working in therapy.

Since people need to be motivated for therapy to benefit from it, dragging an unwilling family member or friend into treatment is generally a waste of time and effort. If someone you care about has a problem but is unwilling to seek help, invite them to therapy with you but do not try to force them to come. Whether they come or not, seek help for yourself. You may discover that you are protecting them from their pain and there may be things you can do which will cause the other person enough pain so that they will seek help. But there are no guarantees.

You may very well begin therapy by trying to change others. It is very likely that in the beginning of therapy, you will be more interested in getting others to change than in making changes in yourself.

Form a therapy triangle. It will be natural for you to form an alliance with your therapist which will not include important family members. This alliance of yourself and your therapist in the presence of your powerful ties to your important family members will cause the therapy triangle to form. How maturely you, your therapist, and your family handle this triangle will determine the outcome of therapy.

Eventually, even reluctantly, **begin to work on yourself.** Making lasting changes is difficult because there is stiff opposition to change both from yourself and from others who are close to you. Strong forces will pull you towards staying the way you are. Lasting change is hard, but not impossible.

Find a mature, well-differentiated therapist. Therapists are people; some are wiser and more mature than others. Wise and mature therapists, those who are most "differentiated", are the most helpful therapists, regardless of their area of specialization, the type of therapy they practice, their gender, their race, or their age. These well-differentiated therapists do not take sides in the therapy triangle and they inspire you to improve yourself, rather than to blame others. Wise and mature therapists are not easy to find but they are the ones who can help you to make lasting changes.

Work on becoming more differentiated by working on two intertwining aspects of your life: your self and your connections with others. Shift your attention away from blaming and changing others and towards understanding and changing your own thoughts, feelings, and reactions. This shift involves taking responsibility for your self and being responsible to others rather than feeling responsible for others. It involves a difficult and life-long process of sorting through what is really important for you to do with your life.

Work on making and maintaining relatively non-anxious connections with important others in your life, especially the members of your nuclear and extended families. "Non-anxious connections" are ones in which you are able to calmly make clear to others where you stand on important issues without trying to coerce them to agree with you. In order to make and maintain non-anxious connections, you may need to extract yourself from between two parties who are in conflict with each other and, at the same time, maintain non-anxious connections with both parties. Making progress in defining your self and making your connections less anxious means that you will raise your level of differentiation.

Even after your pain is gone, work hard to maintain the changes you have made. **Don't stop therapy when you have just begun to feel better.** Stick with it for some time after your symptoms and pain are gone and you will be less likely to relapse and much more likely to make lasting changes in your life.

Use therapeutic techniques and psychiatric medication to help improve your level of differentiation, but remember that things can get worse when you get better. There are many therapeutic techniques and many psychiatric medications which may help you by reducing the power that your problems have over your life. The result is that you will feel more in control of your life. These "improvements" in your life can lead either to lasting change or, ironically, to keeping you stuck in old patterns. Only if the reduction in your symptoms leads you to increase your level of differentiation will you make lasting changes. It is that simple and that difficult.

Work hard at not letting logistical problems get in the way. In your search for professional help, you are likely to encounter many logistical problems such as finding a good therapist, deciding who should go to therapy with you, deciding when to change therapists, deciding how long to stay in therapy, figuring out how you can afford therapy, and finding the time for it. These problems can prevent you from making lasting changes. However, you can often overcome these problems with persistence and assertiveness. You might be tempted to blame logistical problems for the failure of your therapy; work hard to overcome those problems.

If you are even moderately successful in making changes by increasing your level of differentiation, your changes will be very rewarding. You will experience more inner peace and a renewed sense of accomplishment. You will have more clarity about yourself and more success in acting on your values and your purposes in life. You will experience increased closeness with those you value and increased tolerance for those you don't. You will have a stronger psychological immune system which will help you deal more effectively with future loss and trauma. You might even see growth in those "others" around you, the members of your extended and nuclear family, particularly if you work on yourself rather than on them.

I wish you well in all your therapeutic endeavors. Go forth and do great things!

BIBLIOGRAPHY

Bowen, Murray, *Family Systems Theory in Clinical Practice*. New York: Jason Aronson, 1978.
> A collection of Dr. Bowen's papers on his theory. Difficult going for the non-professional but an excellent source book on differentiation and emotional triangles.

Burns, David D., M.D., *Feeling Good: The New Mood Therapy*. New York: Penguin, 1980.
> An excellent book about cognitive therapy for depression and anxiety written for the layperson.

Kerr, Michael and Bowen, Murray, *Family Evaluation*. New York: Norton, 1988.
> The best and most complete exposition of Bowen's theory. Not easy reading and understanding but worth the work if you want an in-depth understanding of Differentiation and emotional triangles.

Friedman, Edwin, *Generation to Generation: Family Process in Church and Synagogue*. New York: Guilford Press, 1985.
> An intriguing and insightful application of Bowen's theory to therapy and to religious organizations by one of Dr. Bowen's most lucid and entertaining disciples.

Friedman, Edwin, *Friedman's Fables.* New York: Guilford Press, 1985

> A light-hearted but profound look at family sytems theory.

Lerner, Harriet, Ph.D., *The Dance of Anger: A Woman's Guide to Changing the Patterns of Intimate Relationships.* New York: Harper and Row, 1985.

> A powerful explanation for the lay reader of how patterns of relationships influence women and how those patterns can be changed. Lerner does an excellent job of applying some of Murray Bowen's ideas to the everyday relationship problems of women.

Papero, Daniel, *Bowen's Family Systems Theory.* Boston: Allyn and Bacon, 1990.

> A solid and relatively brief summary of Bowen's theory including good chapters on differentiation and triangles.

ABOUT THE AUTHOR

Dr. Burkham was born and raised in St. Louis, Missouri, graduated from Princeton University (A.B., 1971), and earned his Ph.D. in Clinical Psychology from St. Louis University in 1981. He has lived and practiced in Appleton, Wisconsin since 1982.

More information regarding psychotherapy and Dr. Burkham's practice is available at www.therapytriangle.com.

NOTES

NOTES

Empowering you with the knowledge to heal

NOTES

NOTES

NOTES

NOTES

NOTES

NOTES

NOTES

NOTES

NOTES